A GUIDE TO MEDICAID HOME CARE IN NEW YORK

How to Beat the System at Its Own Game to Get the Care You or Your Loved One Needs

Lori R. Somekh, Esq.

Illustrations by Jim Sarlis, Esq.

"The most terrifying words in the English language are... 'I'm from the government & I'm here to help you.'"

- Ronald Reagan

Dedication

To all my colleagues and luminaries out there in the trenches, fighting the good fight to keep elderly and disabled people in their homes, against the weight of the crushing attempts to shrink the home and community-based services in New York.

Contents

Introduction | Am I Having A Nervous Breakdown?

"A fundamental concern for others in our individual and community lives would go a long way in making the world the better place we so passionately dreamt of."

- Nelson Mandela

The rising sun casts long shadows in the quiet suburban neighborhood, heralding another day of ceaseless anxiety for Emily. Every morning, she juggles her career with a disheartening and confusing task - securing the services of home health aides for her aging father under the New York Medicaid home care program. Her life has transformed into a balancing act, between managing work, personal life, and her father's health needs, a demanding array of responsibilities that are becoming increasingly stressful.

She feels as if her life is spinning out of control, and Emily isn't sure where to turn for help. She feels like she's on the verge of a nervous breakdown?

As a program designed to provide long-term care services to those in need, the New York Medicaid home care program seems like a beacon of hope at first glance. Yet, the path to securing these services can be strewn with obstacles and complexities that are daunting for an already overwhelmed caregiver like Emily.

From understanding the eligibility criteria, such as age, residency, income, and the amount of care needed, to gathering the necessary documentation for the application, each step involves plowing through a web of red tape. Information is often buried deep within lengthy policy documents, hidden behind layers of legal jargon and conflicting information, rendering comprehension impossible. A constant loop of phone calls, paperwork, and interviews, while dealing with the bureaucratic machinery, becomes an integral part of Emily's daily life, adding to her growing stress load.

Further amplifying her anxiety is the need for a comprehensive medical examination by a state-approved nurse and then a state-approved doctor; a process that can take weeks to schedule and complete. The results are then presented to a faceless panel; a group of individuals who have never met her father, to decide whether his needs are “severe” enough or “stable” enough for home care. The fear of rejection and the uncertainty of her father’s future loom ominously over Emily like a dark cloud.

The entire process seems very non-transparent. The scarce guidance available makes it even harder for an already burdened Emily, leaving her feeling alone and unsupported. The system, though well-intentioned, seems to have overlooked the fact that the individuals seeking its help are often those most in need of compassion, understanding, and assistance.

In addition to the complex system, Emily grapples with the emotional strain of ensuring her father's well-being. The pressure of finding trustworthy, reliable home health aides who will treat her father with the respect and dignity he deserves is immense. She is haunted by the ever-present concern for her father's safety and well-being, adding to the pressure she feels.

Despite these challenges, Emily, like countless others, endures. She wades through the bureaucratic maze day after day, armed with nothing but her love for her father and the desperate hope for some help. The need to maintain her career, the desire to ensure her father's comfort and the daunting task of battling a complex system weighs heavily on her shoulders. But she fights on, fueled by determination and deep, unyielding love. This struggle may be Emily's story, but it is also the story of countless adult children battling stress and adversity in their quest to provide their aging parents the care they need and deserve.

This book is your companion in this battle. Written by an experienced elder law attorney, it will help you find your way through the maze of the New York Medicaid home care program. It provides comprehensive guidance about eligibility criteria, application procedures, and other related matters. You will learn how to navigate the system efficiently and secure the best possible care for your loved one. You probably won't want to do it yourself, but it will give you a better understanding of some of the nuances of the process, so you will have an idea of what the journey looks like and will be able to manage your expectations. So, instead of walking into a dark tunnel with no idea what the end looks like, you'll be able to prepare yourself with a realistic goal in mind.

You are not alone. The author, Lori, will provide guidance and insights throughout this journey to help you make the best decisions for your loved one's care. Read on, and know that you do not have to go through this process alone. There are resources out there and this is one time that it may pay to ask for help.

Let's embark on this journey together!

Author's Note

I've written this book because I want to pull back the curtain on how to access Medicaid home care in New York and to dispel the widespread belief that people can't get full-time care in their homes through Medicaid. Although we routinely get full-time care in place for our high-needs clients, I'm constantly hearing from people who can't get the right amount of care for their loved ones and do not even realize full-time care is available.

I've been practicing in this field for long enough that I've heard way too many stories about people who have lost their jobs or have had to quit their jobs because they can't get enough help taking care of a sick or infirm parent. I've heard so many stories about people not being able to get more than six hours a day of care for a parent who is bed-bound and lives alone. I recently had a physician tell me he's never seen a patient get more than six hours a day!

Honestly, I'm appalled. Now, make no mistake - people aren't pulling these ideas out of thin air. They are experiencing this failure of our long-term care system first-hand. When I speak to prospective clients who are trying to get care in place for their mom or dad, more often than not, the person on the other end of the phone already sounds defeated. They're usually surprised to learn that they are eligible for - and can get - full-time, round-the-clock aides for their mom or dad. I often speak to people with a bed-bound parent who lives alone and has been given an aide for six hours a day, and the son or daughter has to go there when the aide leaves and spend the night there, getting up in the middle of the night when the parent needs something. Then, they have to get up the next morning and go to work. Almost always, the family has asked for an increase in hours and has been denied. They've often requested a plan appeal, and that has also been denied.

The tragedy here is that many people simply believe that more care is not available. And this is where the process ends for them.

This reveals a couple points of failure. The first failure is that the system is confusing, and many people are not correctly informed about what they are able to receive. Many people research on the internet and get all kinds of conflicting information. Despite the efforts by the Elder Law Bar to do outreach to educate consumers, there are still widespread misconceptions about how the home care system works. And the Managed Long-Term Care ("MLTC") plans are complicit in perpetuating many of the misconceptions. My clients are regularly told by their plans that they are not entitled to receive the number of hours they are requesting when, in fact, they are.

Another failure is disparities based on the way consumers enter into the home care system. There is not one method of applying for Medicaid home care. Some people apply through a care agency, some apply through an MLTC plan, and some with the assistance of their doctor's office or a nursing home discharge planner. There are many doors through which people can come into the system. However, not all approaches yield the same result. If you apply through any of these doors, you will likely get six hours. Therefore, it is necessary to have a strategy in place from the beginning and plan out how you will apply in order to get the best result and get it in the quickest amount of time. That's how we approach the home care process with our clients—strategically.

Another failure is that, very often, families believe that they cannot get *what the MLTC tells them they cannot get*. Then, when a person asks for a plan appeal, they are asking the Plan to reverse its own decision. Although it sometimes does happen, the usual result is that the Plan agrees with its original decision, or they may give an extra hour a day on appeal - so they'll give 7 hours a day instead of 6. Once the plan gives them a negative decision on appeal, people often think it's over. It's understandable how they conclude that, because, although the plans give written decisions on these appeals, they *always* call the client on the phone and tell them verbally that they've been denied. The dejected client might not even read the letter that comes in the mail often weeks later. This is not to say that family members never read the follow-up letter they eventually get in the mail and see that they are entitled to further appeals. Sometimes, they do, and those are the people who might call our office and get help.

What many clients don't know is that their chances on the next levels of appeal are pretty good.

First, I'm going to give you an overview of the home care program in New York and get a little into the weeds about how things work. Then I'll go over how to approach the home care request strategically, so you have a good shot at getting the right amount of care in the first place. Lastly, I'll explain how we appeal when we don't have sufficient hours.

A word of caution: Do not beat yourself up if you are utterly confused by this process. It wasn't designed to be user-friendly. I'm not trying to be cynical and suggest the program is a mess intentionally – it's not. It just has way too many moving parts. My clients usually feel the same way I do when I'm trying to tackle something I have no expertise in, such as anything tech-related. It's just incomprehensible to me no matter how hard I try to figure it out, because it is not something I'm familiar with.

Conventions: For purposes of readability and acceptable use of pronouns, the terms "their", "they", and "them" are used rather than "he", "him", "his", or "she", "her", "hers".

Chapter 1 | Overview of the Medicaid Home Care Process in New York

By default, we have created a "system" of nursing-home care for the aged in which middle-class people pay exorbitant rates to for-profit nursing-home entrepreneurs – and then when private resources are consumed and the patient qualifies as a pauper, the nursing home begins billing Medicaid. This is precisely the antithesis of social citizenship; instead of the poor being accorded the dignity associated with the middle class, equality of treatment is achieved by making the middle class undergo pauperization."

- Robert Kuttner

Why Medicaid?

People often get confused about why they would ever end up on Medicaid when they've worked their whole lives and are not experiencing poverty. Most people know that Medicaid is a joint federal and state program that provides health coverage and long-term care services to individuals who have limited income and assets.

Unfortunately, in the United States, our Medi**care** system does not pay for extended stays in a rehabilitation facility or a nursing home. Neither do private insurance plans. Therefore, people are often surprised to learn that if their loved one needs long-term care in a nursing home or rehabilitation facility, it must be paid for out of pocket - i.e., private pay. Medi**care** also doesn't pay for home health aides to take care of people in their own homes. That is also private pay.

That's why we have no choice but to look to Medicaid to come in and fill in the gap. This wasn't the original purpose of Medicaid when it came into being in 1965. It was intended as a safety net for people living at or near the poverty level. But by necessity, it has grown into the way we care for seniors and disabled people in this country.

Over the years, a whole regulatory system has been developed, with exemptions and loopholes and safe harbors (kind of like the tax code) to let us legally get people "broke" so they can get this type of care paid for through Medicaid. There are ways to transfer assets and shelter income so that people can qualify for these benefits without actually becoming destitute. This is done not to game the system, but to prevent families from depleting their life's savings when they have a family member who needs long-term care (for example, so the well spouse doesn't end up homeless). But, to avoid this consequence, you really need to know the rules, and they are complex (not unlike the tax rules). And there's plenty of opportunity for the unwary to be misled and end up losing a lot of money or suffering with inadequate care that could have been avoided by understanding and following the rules.

The Medicaid home care program in New York is designed to provide in-home care services to individuals who are elderly, disabled or blind and need assistance in order to remain in their homes. This program can be an important resource for those who need help with activities of daily living, such as bathing, dressing, walking, showering, using the bathroom and meal preparation.

In addition to meeting specific criteria, applicants must also collect a variety of documents and complete numerous forms. The required paperwork can include pay stubs, bank statements, birth certificates, marriage or divorce papers, Social Security statements, and more. It is also necessary to provide detailed information about one's current living situation as well as any medical diagnoses or prescription medications they have.

The application process can be further complicated by the sheer volume of information that must be gathered and the confusing language and instructions used in the forms. For those who are unfamiliar with Medicaid regulations, understanding eligibility criteria and completing paperwork can be a little overwhelming, adding to the family's stress.

The good news is that there is help available to make this process easier for applicants. A knowledgeable elder law attorney can provide invaluable guidance and assistance throughout the process. They can help navigate the application process, ensuring that all necessary documents are gathered, and the application process is approached strategically.

In this chapter, we will provide an overview of the big picture of what you can expect as you navigate the process of getting into the Medicaid home care program in New York.

In New York, the program is known as Home Care Services Program ("HCSP"). It is administered by the state Department of Health ("DOH") and provides in-home personal care services ("PCS") for those who meet specific eligibility criteria. It is important to note that the Medicaid home care program is a needs-based program, meaning that individuals must meet specific eligibility requirements in order to receive benefits. These requirements include citizenship or legal residency, residency in New York State, and limited income and assets. Additionally, individuals must require assistance with at least two activities of daily living ("ADLs") or one if there is a dementia diagnosis.

This program can be a vital resource for families who are caring for a loved one who needs help with activities of daily living. With the Medicaid home care program, these individuals can receive the care they need in the comfort of their own homes, rather than in a nursing home or other long-term care facility.

Navigating the application process for Medicaid home care in New York can be intimidating. Knowledge and preparation will help you get your loved one the care they need and deserve. In this book, we will provide the information and guidance necessary to make this process as seamless as possible, so that you can focus on what's most important- providing the best care for your loved one.

Step 1 | Determine Eligibility

The first step in the process of getting a loved one enrolled in the Medicaid home care program is to determine their eligibility. This step is critical, as only individuals who meet specific eligibility requirements will be able to receive benefits through the program.

New York has passed new regulations requiring that an individual must need assistance with three ADLs, or two if there is a dementia diagnosis, but the implementation of the new regulations has been delayed by federal directives related to the COVID emergency and recovery. At the time of this writing, we do not know when these new rules will go into effect. At this moment, an individual must need help with two ADLs and one if there is a dementia diagnosis.

To determine your loved one's eligibility, you will need to gather information and documentation about their citizenship or legal residency status, residency in New York State, and financial situation. This information will be used to determine their specific eligibility for the Medicaid home care program.

The specific eligibility requirements will be discussed in Chapter 2.

Step 2 | Gather Information & Documents

Once you have determined that your loved one is eligible for the Medicaid home care program, the next step is to gather all the necessary information and documents that will be used to determine their specific eligibility and the level of care they need.

It is essential to gather accurate and complete information to ensure that the Medicaid home care application process goes smoothly and that your loved one receives the care they require based on their unique circumstances and needs.

The information and documents you will need to gather may include:

- ❖ Proof of residency in New York State
- ❖ Proof of U.S. citizenship or legal residency
- ❖ Financial information, including proof of all sources of income, bank statements and tax returns (TIP: When providing bank statements, include all pages, even blanks.)
- ❖ Medical information, including doctor's reports and medical histories

Proof of residency in New York State is necessary to ensure that your loved one is eligible for the Medicaid home care program, as it is only available to residents of the state. Proof of U.S. citizenship or legal residency is also required, such as a birth certificate, passport or naturalization papers. Financial information, including bank statements and tax returns, will be used to determine an individual's financial eligibility for the program. Medical information, such as doctors' reports and medical histories, is necessary to assess the individual's specific needs and determine what level of care they require. All this information must be provided in order to move forward with the application process.

There are also several forms you will need to complete for the home care assessments. Home care assessments, also known as needs assessments, are a critical component of the Medicaid home care application process, arguably the most important. These assessments use information collected from both the applicant and their doctor to help determine an individual's specific care needs and what type of services they may qualify for.

Using this information, the assessor will be able to make recommendations about the appropriate level of care and services the individual needs. It is a good idea to start gathering this information as soon as possible, as some of it may take time to obtain. You will do well to have an attorney's office and a care manager assist you in these assessments, because this is where there is a big opportunity to advocate for the amount of care your loved one really needs.

Step 3 | Complete the Application

With all the required information and documents gathered, the next step in the Medicaid home care process is to complete the application. This step is where all the information and documentation you have gathered will be used to determine your loved one's specific eligibility for the program and the level of care they will receive.

The information and documents gathered in the previous step will need to be submitted along with the completed application form. It is a good idea to review all the documents carefully before submitting them to avoid any delays in processing. Additionally, it is important to note that any false statements on the application may lead to future problems. (TIP: Have your attorney's office handle this for you.)

The Local Department of Social Services ("LDSS"), responsible for determining eligibility, will then review all the information provided in order to make a decision about whether or not your loved one qualifies for home care services, as well as what type and level of care they are eligible for. This can be a lengthy process, but we have strategies that may shortcut the process significantly.

Part of the application process will include obtaining medical documentation from the patient's doctor, typically pursuant to a new medical appointment. Your loved one's doctor or nurse practitioner may also need to complete a medical form to be submitted with the application. This is an important step in ensuring that all the necessary information has been provided to determine eligibility and that the individual's care needs are accurately reflected in the application.

Step 4 | Await Approval

Once the Medicaid home care application has been submitted, the next step is to await approval. This can be a stressful time, as you wait to hear whether your loved one will be able to receive the care they need through the Medicaid home care program. The approval process can take from several weeks to several months, depending on the complexity of the case, *the way you apply*, and the current backlog of applications. There are also often ways of getting this process expedited.

Once the application has been reviewed and a decision has been made, you will be notified, in writing, of the outcome. When the application is approved, you will be able to proceed to the next step of having assessments completed to determine how much and what type of care is needed and ultimately begin receiving services. (Again, this process may be expedited depending on our method of applying).

An application for Medicaid home care may be denied for a variety of reasons, including insufficient medical and financial documentation, inaccurate or incomplete information on the application, failure to meet program eligibility requirements, or being over the asset threshold. Additionally, if an individual's care needs exceed the scope of services covered by the program, an application may also be denied. In these cases, it is important to consult with an elder law attorney who can help you appeal the decision if appropriate and gather additional information and documentation to support your loved one's eligibility. Appeals will be discussed in Chapter Nine.

During the review process, the LDSS may send you requests for additional information. These requests are made in writing. They may be titled "Request for Information" or "Notice of Deferral" or something else. It is critical that you open any mail from the LDSS immediately and provide the requested information right away. These letters will always have a deadline. If you cannot obtain the requested information by the deadline, you must request an extension; otherwise, you will receive a denial.

Step 5 | Assessments

Once the application is approved, there are several assessments that must take place.

During a home care assessment, a nurse assessor will ask questions about the individual's health, functional abilities, living situation, daily activities, ability to participate in self-care tasks such as bathing or dressing themselves, and any other factors that may affect their ability to live independently. The assessor will also review medical records and physician reports to get a better understanding of the person's condition.

This is a process fraught with mine fields and will be discussed in Chapter 3.

Step 6 | Begin Receiving Services

If your loved one's Medicaid home care application is approved and the necessary assessments have taken place, the next step is to begin receiving services. This is the step where your loved one will be able to start receiving the care and support they need to live comfortably and safely at home.

The specific services that your loved one will receive will be determined based on their individual needs and the Medicaid home care program they are enrolled in. These typically include personal care services, such as help with bathing and grooming, and assistance with activities of daily living, such as housekeeping and meal preparation.

It is important to work closely with the Department of Social Services and the Medicaid home care provider to ensure that your loved one is receiving the services they need and that their care plan is being followed. If you are being assisted by an elder law attorney, you will likely have a care manager to ensure that your loved one is receiving the highest quality and right amount of care.

A care manager is a professional who works with seniors and their families to coordinate services, ensure that their rights are being upheld and advocate for their best interests. Care managers typically have experience in health and social services, as well as extensive knowledge of the Medicaid home care program. They will typically participate in many of the assessments to be sure the patient's needs are being conveyed accurately so they get sufficient hours.

Receiving care in their own home can help your loved one maintain their independence, privacy, and dignity; in addition, being able to remain at home typically reduces the risk of infection and is less disruptive to routines. Finally, receiving care in a familiar environment can be comforting and reassuring for both you and your loved one.

Getting a loved one enrolled in the Medicaid home care program in New York and beginning to receive services is the first point of relief in a confusing process. With the right information and guidance, you can minimize (albeit not eliminate) the pain of the process.

Chapter 2 | Eligibility Criteria

The Medicaid program in New York has specific eligibility criteria. In this chapter, we will discuss the steps involved in determining if you or your loved one is eligible for the Medicaid home care program.

There are three ways in which applicants for home care must qualify:

1. **Applicant must qualify income-wise:**

   - Income must be no more than $1,677.00 per month for a single person and $2,268 for a married couple (as of 1/1/23). The threshold for both income and assets changes every January. If the income exceeds the threshold, the person can join a pooled income trust to shelter the surplus.

2. **Applicant must qualify asset-wise:**

   - Assets must be no more than $30,182.00 for a single person and $40,821 for a married couple (as of 1/1/23).

   - If the assets exceed the threshold, assets must be transferred (in a proper way) in order to qualify for Medicaid. There is no lookback period for Medicaid home care as of this writing. A 30-month lookback period is on the books in New York, but it has not yet been implemented, for various reasons.

3. **Applicant must qualify medically:**

   - Applicant must require assistance with some activities of daily living. Additionally, to be eligible to use a pooled income trust, a person must have been determined to be disabled.

Clients often confuse the income and asset criteria. Medicaid considers these categories separately. For example, as will be discussed in a later chapter, we often shelter excess income in a pooled income trust, and that is handled on a monthly basis. Income is addressed at the time of the application.

A pooled income trust is a tool used by individuals who have too much income to qualify for Medicaid home care, but not enough to pay for their own care. It allows surplus income to be deposited into an account that is managed by an authorized agency, and the funds are then used to pay the individual's bills. The advantage of this type of trust is that the person who has too much monthly income can still qualify for Medicaid and not have to contribute the excess income toward the cost of the care.

Income refers to what you receive monthly, such as Social Security, pension, IRA distributions, dividends and rental income. Assets, on the other hand, are things like real property, bank accounts, investment accounts, annuities, CDs and the cash value of whole life insurance. These must often be removed from the applicant's name, and we may use vehicles such as a Medicaid Asset Protection Trust for this.

A Medicaid Asset Protection Trust is a legal tool used to protect assets for those who are applying for Medicaid home care. This type of trust enables individuals to transfer their assets into an irrevocable trust, which allows them to qualify for Medicaid. This type of trust requires careful planning and should only be done with assistance from an elder law attorney so that all rules and regulations are correctly followed. Do NOT do this by yourself!

People often get confused about the need to deal with two trusts, one for income, and one for assets, but they each serve separate functions and are often both necessary.

Another thing that people typically ask is whether they can appoint a friend or family member to be the trustee of the pooled income trust. A trustee is a person or entity that is responsible for managing the assets in another person's trust. The trustee is responsible for making sure that all funds are used in accordance with the trust's terms and conditions and following all applicable laws and regulations. The trustee also has a fiduciary responsibility to ensure that the beneficiary of the trust receives maximum benefit from its assets.

Although a person can choose a friend or family member to act as trustee of the Medicaid Asset Protection Trust (which is used to shield the assets), that is not the case for the pooled income trust. The pooled income trust must be managed by one of the approved pooled income trust organizations in New York. There are a handful of pooled income trusts in New York that handle the administration of these trusts. People often don't like the idea of this, but once they get set up with the pooled trust, the process usually works like clockwork.

To use a pooled income trust, an individual must be disabled. In order to be considered disabled, an individual must have a physical or mental impairment that has lasted (or is expected to last) at least 12 months and that renders them unable to do any substantial gainful activity. A significant number of medical conditions can satisfy this requirement, including chronic illnesses such as cancer, HIV/AIDS, muscular dystrophy, multiple sclerosis and many others. In addition, certain developmental disabilities may also qualify. Each application will need to include sufficient medical evidence in order to satisfy the Medicaid requirements for disability. This will typically include the applicant's medical records from doctors and other providers who know about their condition(s). This will be discussed further in chapter 5.

Chapter 3 | The Many Programs & Assessments

There are a number of different home care programs and many assessments that must be completed in order to qualify for Medicaid home care. These programs include: the Managed Long-Term Care ("MLTC") program and the New York Home and Community-Based Services Waivered Programs (which include the Nursing Home Transition and Diversion ("NHTD") and Traumatic Brain Injury ("TBI") programs).

The required assessments include: New York Independent Assessor ("NYIA") Assessments, Immediate Needs Assessments and MLTC Assessments. There are also assessments required for the NHTD and TBI waivered programs. All these assessments have specific purposes.

Programs

The MLTC program is a statewide program administered by the New York State Department of Health and is the primary way home care is delivered in New York. It operates under a managed care paradigm, as opposed to a fee-for-service paradigm. Under managed care, the plan gets a flat fee for each person on its rolls rather than being paid for the actual services provided. This will be discussed further in Chapter 9.

The New York Home and Community-Based Services Waivered Programs are programs that provide services and supports to people who are in need of long-term care and who meet certain criteria. It is also designed to help individuals remain living independently in the community instead of being placed in a nursing home or other facility.

In order to be eligible for these programs, an individual must meet specific criteria that include age, type of disability (such as dementia, stroke or traumatic brain injury), income, and other requirements.

Assessments

NYIA Assessments are mandatory independent assessments completed by a nurse and a nurse practitioner or physician, respectively, who evaluate the suitability of an applicant for Medicaid home care. The assessor will look at the individual's current health status, medical history, and functional abilities and determine if home care is appropriate.

Immediate Needs Assessments are completed by nurse assessors to determine if an individual requires immediate care and services. The Immediate Needs Assessment evaluates the individual's physical, mental, emotional, and social needs, as well as their ability to carry out activities of daily living such as bathing, dressing, and eating.

MLTC Assessments are completed by nurse assessors who use an assessment tool called the Uniform Assessment System – New York. This tool assesses several areas, such as physical function, cognitive ability, social functioning, and psychological health. These assessments are used to formulaically determine how much care the plan will authorize.

Chapter 4 | What if I Have Too Much Money?

For reasons discussed in Chapter 1, there is currently no specifically designed system in place for payment for long-term care in the United States. The resulting dilemma is that payment for long-term care defaults to the Medicaid program. However, if a person has too much money or too much in assets, they may not qualify for Medicaid. But this doesn't mean that we can't get them qualified. Because every individual's financial situation is unique, it makes sense to work with an elder law attorney to explore different options so you can receive the home care services you need.

Many seniors who would not have ever been candidates for means-tested programs will find themselves needing to avail themselves of the Medicaid program in their "golden years". And in such cases, people do not start out being eligible for Medicaid. Often, we have to make them eligible.

One method of doing this may be setting up a certain type of trust. A trust can be used to hold assets from the applicant for the benefit of a third party, such as a family member or other trusted individual, in order to reduce the value of an applicant's estate so they no longer have too many resources. This process can help individuals who have assets in excess of Medicaid's asset limit but still need home care services, while also helping them preserve some of their financial resources. Your attorney will make sure that this process is done correctly and does not create more problems than it solves.

Another way of making someone eligible is through gifting. Transferring assets to a third party, such as a family member or another trusted person, can help reduce the value of an applicant's estate so they no longer have too much money or too much in assets and are able to qualify for Medicaid. However, this is not always a good idea. Once money is transferred to someone, it is legally the other person's property. If you need to get it back for some reason, that person is not legally obligated to return it. That money also may be exposed to the other person's creditors, should they be sued. It may also pass to the other person's heirs should they die—so this action must be carefully considered.

It is important to note that these transactions must be done in accordance with Medicaid regulations, so it is best to discuss this option with a knowledgeable attorney. If done incorrectly, gifting can actually harm your chances of becoming Medicaid eligible.

Therefore, estate planning can be an important first step to take. Estate planning puts you in control of your assets and property and helps make sure that the people you care about are taken care of after you have passed away or become incapacitated. It also allows you to designate who will manage your affairs if you cannot do so yourself.

By taking the time to plan ahead, applicants can be better prepared to apply for Medicaid home care and ensure they get the care and support they need if the time comes.

Chapter 5 | What if I Have Too Much Income?

Pooled Income Trusts – The Good, The Bad, & The Ugly

How do we shelter income when the applicant makes too much money?

The income threshold for Medicaid eligibility is very low ($1,677/month for a single person and $2,268/month for a married couple in 2023). Many people requiring home care have income in excess of that amount.

For any New Yorker who requires home care and has a disability, a pooled income trust can be used to shelter the excess income. In order to use a pooled trust, a disability determination must be made by the Department of Health, unless the person was already determined to be disabled by the Social Security Administration in the past. This would have only occurred if the person previously applied for disability benefits from Social Security. Medicaid uses the same criteria that the Social Security Administration uses for Social Security Disability.

When it comes to determining whether an individual is disabled, there are certain criteria that must be met. In order to qualify, applicants must demonstrate that their disability or medical condition significantly limits their ability to perform basic activities like walking, lifting, bending and standing. Below are some of the criteria used by the Department of Health in evaluating whether someone has a disability:

- ❖ Inability to engage in any substantial gainful activity by reason of any medically determinable physical or mental impairment which can be expected to result in death or has lasted or can be expected to last for a continuous period of not less than 12 months.

- An inability to do any kind of work that exists in significant numbers in the national economy.

- If blind under the Social Security Act (blindness is defined as central visual acuity 20/200 or less in the better eye with corrective lenses).

- Physical impairments that prevent independent living, such as severe arthritis, stroke, paralysis, and other mobility-impairing conditions.

- Mental impairments such as schizophrenia, dementia, depression, bipolar disorder, anxiety and other psychological conditions that affect daily living activities.

- Developmental disabilities such as autism, cerebral palsy or Downs Syndrome that are likely to continue indefinitely and significantly impair daily functioning.

- Chronic diseases such as HIV/AIDS, cancer or chronic liver disease which cause physical limitations and fatigue.

- Other medical conditions that can prevent a person from performing normal activities of daily living (ADLs) without assistance, including preparing food, bathing and dressing themselves, using the toilet, managing medications, shopping, doing housework, taking public transportation or navigating their neighborhood safely, communicating with others and managing financial matters independently.

The Pooled Income Trust - What is it?

A pooled income trust is a way of making someone with too much *income* eligible for Medicaid. As previously mentioned, Medicaid is a means-tested program, which means recipients must have less than a certain amount of income and resources. Since the income threshold in New York is very low, most middle-income people would not qualify. However, when it comes to getting home health aides for seniors or disabled people, health insurance companies, including Medicare, do not cover this type of health care. So most middle-income people don't qualify for Medicaid but also cannot afford to pay privately for home health aides.

The average cost of a home health aide in the state of New York is approximately $25 -$35 an hour. This rate may vary depending on location and other factors. The cost for home health aides can also be affected by the level of care needed, as more involved services may require a higher fee. Additionally, some agencies may charge extra fees for additional services such as transportation or supplies.

So, for people who cannot afford to privately pay for home health aides, the only alternative is to ask Medicaid to pay for the care. Without this type of care, many seniors and disabled people would not be able to remain in their homes. Fortunately, New York allows people to utilize pooled income trusts as a method of sheltering their surplus income so they can have care and still afford to pay their bills.

Why do I Need One?

You would typically need a pooled income trust if you are receiving Medicaid home care and your income is higher than the Medicaid threshold. This is a very misunderstood concept. The income of seniors may typically be their Social Security retirement, pension, IRA income, income from annuities and possible rental income. This quite often is more than the Medicaid threshold and is why pooled income trusts are frequently used. They are a vehicle to shelter surplus income so the Medicaid recipient doesn't have to pay that surplus income to Medicaid or the agency providing the care, which would leave the recipient without money to pay their bills.

How Does it Work?

Let's say Mrs. Smith has a monthly income of $2,500. We would subtract the Medicaid allowable amount ($1,677) from that amount, plus subtract an extra $20 if Mrs. Smith also has Medicare. For example:

$2,500 Monthly income

- $1,677 Medicaid allowable income

- $20 Medicare disregard

= $803 Surplus income

The $803 remaining is considered Mrs. Smith's surplus income - that is, the amount of monthly income over the limit allowed by Medicaid. This surplus can be paid to Medicaid toward the cost of care minus any Medicaid bills she has incurred, or Mrs. Smith can shelter the surplus by utilizing a pooled income trust, thus allowing her to preserve this income for her bills. (After all, she still has to pay the rent, the utilities, groceries, etc.)

As mentioned earlier, these pooled trusts are community trusts authorized by the state for this purpose. Once Mrs. Smith is joined to the pooled trust, she would begin depositing her monthly surplus (the $803 in this example) into the pool and instructing the trustee which of her bills she wants them to pay with that money. Typical bills might be rent, food, utilities or credit cards. The pooled trust gets paid either a flat fee or a percentage of the surplus each month for doing this work.

We will usually advise our clients to sign an authorization with the pooled trust, allowing them to automatically withdraw money from their account on a certain date each month. This withdrawal is set up to occur on a monthly cycle. This method is helpful for people who want to make sure their bills are being paid on time without having to worry about manually sending a check for the surplus to the pool every month.

Each month, the clients give the trustee the bills to pay. If there are any bills that are the same amount every month, those bills can be automated rather than the client or family member having to fax, email or mail the bills over to the pool. This will eliminate the amount of work the client or family member has to do. If done correctly, this will work like clockwork every month. You do not want to accumulate money in this trust, because upon the death of the beneficiary, any excess money will remain in the pool. Importantly, it cannot be used to pay for your funeral after you die. It can, however, be used to prepay your funeral during your lifetime. It can also be used to prepay funerals for your spouse, your children and their spouses.

Logistics

In order to use a pooled income trust, an individual must first receive a disability determination. This is because the Medicaid program requires proof that someone is disabled before they are eligible to shelter income through a pooled income trust.

This disability determination can be made by the Social Security Administration (SSA). The SSA requires that an individual provide proof of disability in the form of medical records or by Medicaid, doctors' notes, or other forms of documentation. Once this determination is made, a person will then be eligible to join a pooled trust and have their surplus income sheltered. For people who have not previously been on Social Security Disability ("SSD") or Supplemental Security Income ("SSI"), the determination must be made by Medicaid, utilizing the same criteria.

What often causes confusion for applicants is the timing. When the home care application is submitted to Medicaid, the pooled trust and the disability documentation are submitted for approval at the same time.

Three things are actually happening simultaneously when the application is received:

1. Medicaid is determining if the applicant is eligible financially;

2. The Home Care unit of Medicaid is determining if the applicant is eligible medically; and

3. The Department of Health is determining if the applicant can be deemed disabled and is, therefore, eligible to use the pooled income trust to shelter the excess income. (By the time a person needs an aide to assist with activities of daily living, they will typically meet the criteria of being disabled.)

The difficult part is that each of these units has different deadlines within which to make their determinations.

- ❖ Medicaid has 45 days to approve financial eligibility. The process can be expedited if the individual is in immediate need of care. This could be due to a sudden change in health, such as an accident or illness that requires them to receive medical assistance immediately. In this situation, there will always be a period of time during which the client is approved and receiving services, but the pooled trust has not been approved yet.

- The Home Care unit works independently to determine the person's care needs, and in Immediate Needs cases, this happens as soon as the application is filed and often even before eligibility is determined.

- The Department of Health (DOH), on the other hand, has 90 days to make a disability determination (and they very often do not adhere to this deadline).

In many counties, including the New York City counties, once Medicaid finds the applicant is eligible financially and medically, Medicaid approval is issued (even though the Department of Health disability determination will not have been made yet).

I often liken the Medicaid system as a bit of an octopus, with each leg doing its own thing, each limb independent of the others, and unaware that the others even exist. The three different units – Medicaid Eligibility, Home Care, and DOH - operate independently of each other. Until the DOH grants final approval of the disability, the practical effect of this looks something like this: Medicaid sees the case as a "surplus income" case and proceeds to try to collect the surplus income from the consumer. This freaks every single client out. But if you understand the process, it will cause you to have less anxiety when you receive confusing information.

Once the disability approval is eventually issued by the DOH, Medicaid stops classifying the case as a “surplus income” case and reissues the budget with a “0” spenddown. Until that time, the case appears as a “surplus income” case, and any care agencies involved think they are entitled to receive the surplus income. Typically, when an applicant shows the agency that a pooled income trust is being utilized and proof that the surplus had been deposited in the pool, the agency is reassured that Medicaid will pay them the additional amount retroactively after the disability approval is issued. Generally, agencies will start care without collecting the surplus income, as long as the consumer agrees that if the disability approval is ultimately not received, they are responsible for paying the surplus amount to the agency. In order for the client to start receiving care prior to DOH approval, the client is asked to sign an agreement to this effect.

For many individuals and families applying for Medicaid home care, the idea of signing an agreement to pay back excess income should the disability be approved can cause hesitation. From a consumer's perspective, this could appear to be a risky move, since it is impossible to predict whether or not they will qualify for disability approval. Not wanting to take on the risk of having to cover the cost out-of-pocket, some consumers choose to wait until the disability approval is issued before starting care. But this option can be difficult since it means they'd have to forgo receiving necessary care while waiting for the approval, and either a family member would have to provide the care for free, or they would have to pay privately for care in the meantime. This would defeat the purpose of applying through the Immediate Needs Program in the first place.

Ultimately, the applicant has two options:

1. Don't start care until the disability is approved by the DOH; or

2. Sign the agreement and trust that the disability will be approved (and, based on our experience, it always is).

It is rare to see a case where an applicant needs a home health aide, and the DOH does not grant a disability approval (so rare that I've never had one). Your elder law attorney can explain the options.

But…why can't the legs of the octopus work together? At least in the New York City boroughs, the Department of Social Services is much too large and even more bureaucratic. Outdated computer systems, a high volume of cases, and the state's constant attempts to make cuts to the budget have left the program struggling to even maintain the resources it has. In recent years, both the governor and the legislature have placed Medicaid in a vulnerable position by imposing numerous alterations and reductions, causing the bureaucracy to face significant challenges in keeping pace. They actually do pretty well considering all the obstacles they have to overcome.

Chapter 6 | New York Did *What?*

"The Medicaid system currently steers people toward nursing home care. Far more people can be covered in community-based care programs for significantly less."

- Ed Rendell

COVID happened. Although the first cases of SARS–CoV–2 ("COVID-19") appeared in late 2019, the disaster hit New York in earnest in March 2020. At exactly that time, the table was set for some drastic changes in New York's Medicaid home care program.

In February 2020, New York's Governor established the Medicaid Redesign Team (MRT II) to help reduce Medicaid spending and ostensibly improve quality of care. The team was tasked with developing strategies and policies for reforming the state's healthcare system through restructuring service delivery models, reducing costs by using technological advances, modernizing regulations, improving access to care and expanding the use of evidence-based practices.

The MRT II included both public and private sector representatives from a wide range of stakeholders, including providers such as hospitals, nursing homes, physicians, behavioral health professionals and managed care plan executives. What this team did not include, notably, were any members of the Elder Law Bar or advocates for consumers of these Medicaid services who are on the front lines helping this population.

In March 2020, the MRT II submitted a plan to the governor that included over one hundred strategies and recommendations for reforming New York's Medicaid system. The plan focused on addressing market and policy issues related to long-term services and supports; supposedly increasing access to home-based care; modernizing regulations; improving data collection and management; expanding access to telehealth; improving integrated delivery systems; enhancing payment models for providers; and increasing efficiency in Medicaid reimbursement.

The plan also included recommendations specifically related to the state's home care program, including changes in eligibility criteria, cost-sharing arrangements, provider qualifications, rate-setting policies, service array definitions, assessment processes, and service delivery options. The MRT's recommendations on the state's home care program were accepted by Governor Cuomo and included in the April 2020 budget.

Translation: the Governor's MRT II team was tasked with finding $2.5-billion worth of "savings" from the Medicaid program in time for the New York State Budget in April 2020. In three meetings, the team developed and approved a proposal of $2.5 billion in cuts, and it was submitted to the Governor and signed into law.

Amid the height of the coronavirus crisis, the state passed the new budget, including these cuts. Some of the cuts included imposing a 30-month lookback period on home care (which they have not yet been able to implement), increasing the number of activities of daily living a person must require assistance with to qualify for home care (also not implemented yet), and requiring patients to be assessed by independent state-appointed doctors and nurses instead of their own practitioners to determine if they qualify for care.

The $2.5 billion in cuts to the New York State Medicaid program will have a significant impact on applicants and consumers of home care services. Numerous strategies were proposed to reduce Medicaid spending, some of which resulted in tighter eligibility criteria for certain services, such as home care. These changes mean that an applicant may be denied access to home care services if they do not meet the new eligibility requirements.

In addition, these cuts also impacted the rates paid to providers and reimbursement models associated with providing home care services. I'm not sure how these drastic cuts to the Medicaid program could be characterized as "increasing access to home-based care" which was one of the stated goals.

Conversely, the cuts have had a negative impact on access to care. Many providers were forced to reduce their staff or even close due to financial constraints caused by the Medicaid cuts, thus reducing the availability of home care services in many areas of New York State. This was particularly concerning for individuals living in rural areas where access to health care is already limited.

The MRT II's recommendations ultimately resulted, and will increasingly result, in decreased access to and quality of care for consumers of home health services, forcing them to rely on alternative sources of support or assistance that may not be as effective or appropriate for their needs.

On March 18, 2020, the federal government instituted a Public Health Emergency ("PHE"), the effect of which was to prevent the states (for our purposes, New York) from cutting services – including the drastic cuts proposed by the MRT while still receiving emergency funding. This was referred to as "Maintenance of Effort," and it limited New York's ability to make these drastic changes that could adversely affect services or programs funded by federal government funds.[1]

[1] Families First Corona Virus Response Act (FFCRA), Sec. 6008(b)(2), providing no Medicaid recipient may lose their coverage or have their spend down increased after March 18, 2020; and FFCPA 6008(b)(3), stating states may not make eligibility standards, methodologies or procedures for determining eligibility for Medicaid more restrictive than they were on 1/1/20.

Maintenance of Effort ("MOE") is a federal requirement that states must adhere to in order to receive emergency funding from the federal government. The MOE requires states to maintain their current levels of spending on programs funded by the Federal Government for as long as they are receiving emergency funds. This means that while a state is receiving or has not spent federal relief funds, it cannot make the drastic changes that would lower services or programs provided under those funds. States are also prohibited from using these funds to replace existing state revenue sources.

The MOE ensured that essential services were maintained and individuals still had access to needed care despite the dramatic April 2020 budget cuts.

Under MOE, states were obligated to maintain their spending for certain federally funded programs at pre-pandemic levels. As such, New York was unable to carry out some of its drastic cost-cutting measures including those proposed by the MRT II, in order for the state to remain eligible for federal aid.

The MOE clause forced New York to keep existing funding for Medicaid home care in place while still receiving much-needed federal aid during the pandemic. This has been a major factor in preserving access to quality care for many individuals across the state who rely on home care services. It has helped protect vulnerable populations from suffering additional harm due to budget cuts that would have otherwise limited their ability to receive necessary assistance with basic activities of daily living.

According to the Consolidated Appropriations Act (H.R. 2617), these MOE restrictions end in December 2023. Under this Act, the earliest date to implement the new 30-month lookback period and increased ADL requirements is March 2024.

However, a separate MOE requirement was created under the American Rescue Plan Act of 2021 ("ARPA"), also known as the COVID-19 Stimulus Package.[2] This Act extends the deadline for the states to spend the extra COVID money given to them through the ARPA until March 31, 2025. Thus, New York may take until April 2025 to implement these drastic cuts to the Medicaid program. Let's hope for that.

[2] 2 Pub. L. 117-2

Chapter 7 | Do I Need A Care Manager?

"There is no greater gift than caring for another human being."

– Dalai Lama XIV

A care manager is an individual responsible for overseeing a person's care needs and managing the coordination of services. Care managers are usually social workers, nurses, or other health professionals with specialized knowledge and expertise in providing long-term care. They help assess a person's need for home healthcare services, coordinate those services, ensure quality standards are met, and provide ongoing monitoring to ensure appropriate service delivery.

Care managers work together with patients, their families, physicians, and other providers involved in their care to ensure optimal outcomes. They evaluate a patient's needs after receiving treatment and identify any potential care needs that may arise due to changes in the patient's health status. Care managers also offer counseling and education on the importance of self-care and preventive health measures.

The services provided by care managers are essential for those needing home healthcare services, especially in light of the changes in the law. A suitable care manager can help ensure that all necessary criteria for home care eligibility have been met, including verifying that a person's medical need is appropriate and that their physical condition qualifies them for services. Care managers can provide assistance and advocacy with the following:

- ❖ Assessment: A care manager can assess the senior's needs, including their medical, psychological, and social needs. They can also evaluate the home environment to determine what modifications or adaptations may be necessary to ensure the senior's safety and well-being.

- Care Plan: Based on the assessment, a care manager can develop a personalized care plan that outlines the type of care needed, the frequency of care, and the specific services required. The care plan can also include information on local resources and programs that can assist the senior and their family.

- Coordination of Services: A care manager can assist with coordinating the delivery of home care services, including scheduling caregivers, arranging transportation to appointments, and ensuring that medical equipment and supplies are available.

- Monitoring and Advocacy: A care manager can monitor the senior's care to ensure that they are receiving the services they need and that the care plan is being followed. If there are issues or concerns, the care manager can act as an advocate for the senior and their family, working to resolve any problems that arise.

- Education and Support: A care manager can provide education and support to the senior and their family, including information on managing chronic conditions, navigating the healthcare system, and coping with caregiver stress.

In the context of the home care process, care management is an integral piece of the puzzle. The care manager arranges and attends the assessments to interface with the state, the insurance plans and care agencies, advocates for the proper amount of care, and assists clients in choosing the type of care and the best plan for their needs.

Once the assessments are complete and the care has been chosen and approved, clients may choose to continue with the Care Management service if they wish to do so. Generally, this service is beneficial as it provides continuity by having someone to call to address issues that arise with the care or the caregivers. It is especially useful if the consumer has high needs and requires the assistance of more than one aide. Some of the services they can receive are:

- ❖ Weekly or bi-weekly check-in calls or visits
- ❖ Developing a monthly schedule for home health aides; this is particularly useful for consumers using the Consumer Directed Personal Assistance Program, where several aides are alternating shifts.

What often happens is that the clients receive something in the mail, and it is hard for them to know if it's from Medicaid, from the MLTC plan, from NYIA, from the care agency or from some other entity in the mix. It's also hard to know the item's level of importance. For example, if they receive letters from NYIA, they need to get them over to the care manager right away. Acting on one of these letters too early could impact their care hours, and acting too late can affect their ability to choose their own MLTC plan.

Care Management in Conjunction with Consumer-Directed Personnel Assistance Program

The Consumer Directed Personal Assistance Program (CDPAP) is a Medicaid home care option available in New York State. This program allows individuals with disabilities to have more control over their home healthcare services and who provides them. With this program, instead of having a home care agency provide aides, the consumer can directly hire and manage their own aides.

The CDPAP can be beneficial for those needing additional flexibility with their home healthcare services or for those with complex medical needs that require multiple different levels of care throughout the day. Consumers (or their families) are able to hire, train, and manage their own aides.

However, managing the care under the CDPAP program can also be a challenge. Consumers must be organized and able to manage their own care and the schedules of their aides or have a family member who can do so. This includes scheduling shifts, hiring and training aides, tracking hours worked, and making sure all paperwork is completed in a timely manner so the aides can get paid. These can be daunting tasks for someone already dealing with health issues or managing multiple medical appointments.

A care manager can help make this process easier by handling the management of the aides. They can provide guidance on how to properly hire and train aides, develop an effective schedule, and assist with tracking hours worked, submitting the records, collecting documentation from providers, and other related duties.

Care managers can ensure that all aspects of the care are managed effectively and efficiently so that the consumer is receiving the necessary care in an organized manner. This allows for a smoother transition into home healthcare services and peace of mind knowing that their care is being properly managed.

Care Managers can address issues between the client, the family, and the care agency (e.g., changing the aide if the consumer is not satisfied).

There are a variety of reasons why a consumer may not be satisfied with their aides. The aides may be unable to provide the level of care needed, have trouble coordinating their schedules, or have difficulty following and understanding directions. The consumer may also feel that the aide is too authoritative, impatient, or unresponsive to their needs. In any case, communication between the consumer and the aide is key, and if this is lacking, then it could result in dissatisfaction on both sides. Additionally, consumers may be looking for an aide who has expertise in certain medical conditions such as dementia or Parkinson's Disease. It should be noted, however, that any change of agency should only be done in close consultation with the care manager or the attorney's office to be sure it does not result in an inadvertent reduction of hours.

A care manager can assist with providing support to both the consumer and aide in order to improve communication. We find a care manager gets called on frequently to intervene on issues among the aides. Often, there's a pecking order that develops, and it usually manifests as disputes over who covers which shifts. It's very helpful for the care manager to handle these situations to keep the stress off the client and the family. They can help mediate conversations between the client, the family, and the care agency in order to find a better solution that works for everyone. This could include swapping out aides or making sure they receive additional training.

The care manager may be utilized to assist a family member in determining if a doctor appointment or hospital visit is needed or assist with changing agencies, if necessary.

All of these services can help reduce stress and allow consumers to focus on their health instead of worrying about administrative tasks. In short, care managers provide an invaluable service that helps ensure consumers receive the best possible care in an organized manner.

Chapter 8 | Preparing Yourself for Success Before Care is Needed

There are steps you can take to give yourself the best chance of having a successful experience. Making sure your finances are in order, decluttering your living space, taking advantage of the assistance available to you when you need it, preparing for assessments ahead of time, having your medical documentation organized and prepared, using a care manager, and finally, managing your expectations on how the process is going to look will all help you navigate the home care process.

Have your Finances in Order

It is essential to speak with an elder law attorney to make sure your loved one is eligible prior to applying, as Medicaid has restrictions on the amount of assets a person can hold and receive benefits. An elder law attorney will be able to advise you on how best to address your finances, what kind of transfers won't affect your eligibility, and other strategies that can help protect your assets while still allowing you access to much-needed home health care services.

That said, it is generally a good idea to consolidate the accounts of a senior who has many accounts in many different locations. I recommend beginning this process as early as possible, preferably before care is needed, because dealing with opening and closing accounts can take more time than expected. If you wait until care is needed, you could experience significant delay and stress. It takes a lot of time to open and close and transfer accounts – more than you'd expect. I have clients who have taken over a year finding and consolidating their parents' accounts. It is often harder than meets the eye.

Declutter if Necessary

Decluttering a living space not only makes it more pleasant and easier to navigate, but it can also be beneficial to a home care application. When an assessment team is sent out, they need to observe the environment in which you are living and ensure that it is safe and suitable for the level of care you require. This means having a clear path of movement throughout the house as well as being able to access necessary medical equipment or supplies quickly and easily. And, in any event, a good cleanout will probably make it easier to locate necessary documents when the time for home care does arrive.

Additionally, having less clutter will help save time during assessments so that more attention can be focused on your specific care needs. In short, decluttering will benefit your home care application by making it easier for assessors to evaluate your situation and determine what kind of services would best serve you.

Get as Much Help with the Process as you need

Hiring an elder law attorney or Medicaid attorney to handle the process may seem quite expensive; some people do prefer to try to navigate the process on their own. Should the process become too overwhelming, you may want to let an attorney's office handle it. Some elder law firms will handle this process for a one-time, flat fee; others do it on an hourly basis. Unfortunately, due to the number of moving parts within the system, as well as the many changes that have been put in place over the recent years, the process can be fraught with delays and possibly time-wasting mistakes. These time delays are not without cost – both in terms of time, money and aggravation, so you want to weigh the cost associated with hiring help and not hiring help.

Prepare for Assessments Ahead of Time

It is important to prepare for assessments ahead of time by making sure the living space is presentable, that all medical documents are organized and ready to be reviewed, and that any questions you may have are answered.

Have Medical Documentation in Order

Requesting and pulling together all your medical documentation in advance will save time during the assessment process and ensure that key information isn't missed or forgotten. This includes doctor's reports, prescriptions and any other documentation pertaining to your medical history. The assessment will go smoother if you do not have to spend time looking for things. In addition to having the documents on hand for assessors to review, it is also important to keep copies of all records in a safe place, as they are often needed for future applications or appeals.

Use a Care Manager

Using a care manager can be immensely beneficial during the assessment process as they have experienced with Medicaid and will know how to advocate for what you need and prevent you from falling into the traps that may cause you to get less care than you actually need. You should not handle the assessments by yourself. I'm talking to the applicant and the adult child here. There are terms of art, buzz words and assessment strategies that you simply don't know if you haven't had experience with this process. And getting this part right from the beginning is key to winning. If you don't get the right care from the beginning, it will cost a lot of time and probably money in legal fees to straighten it out. This is where I tell people not to be penny wise and pound foolish. No judgement—I do the same thing. I'll try to cut corners by doing something myself or hiring the cheapest company, and it ends up costing me double in the end to straighten it out. And I've done this many times over (slow learner).

Manage your expectations

It is crucial to keep in mind that applying for Medicaid home care benefits can take several months from start to finish. It is, therefore, important to manage your expectations. Understanding that no matter how well you prepare, there may still be delays in obtaining approval due to backlogs or other factors outside of our control. Having a team of experienced professionals on your side can help remove a lot of fear and anxiety from the process and can ultimately lead to a more successful result.

To assist in getting your finances in order, you may want to create a "Master Directory" such as the one I use below. Once you've gotten all the information in one place, keep this completed directory with your estate planning documents and other important documents, and let your family know where it is. This will be a helpful guide for your family if something happens to you.

Master Directory

Directory of Assets________________________**Name**____________________________

Bank Account

Company ________ Contact ________________ Phone Number ________________

Account No. ________________ Document Location URL ________________

User Name ________ Password ________________ Amount $ ________________

Bank Account

Company ________ Contact ________________ Phone Number ________________

Account No. ________________ Document Location URL ________________

User Name ________ Password ________________ Amount $ ________________

Bank Account

Company ________ Contact ________________ Phone Number ________________

Account No. ________________ Document Location URL ________________

User Name ________ Password ________________ Amount $ ________________

Bank Account

Company ______ Contact ______ Phone Number ______

Account No. ______ Document Location URL ______

User Name ______ Password ______ Amount $ ______

Brokerage Account

Company ______ Contact ______ Phone Number ______

Account No. ______ Document Location URL ______

User Name ______ Password ______ Amount $ ______

Mutual Fund Account

Company ______ Contact ______ Phone Number ______

Account No. ______ Document Location URL ______

User Name ______ Password ______ Amount $ ______

IRA Account

Company ______ Contact ______ Phone Number ______

Account No. ______ Document Location URL ______

User Name ______ Password ______ Amount $ ______

IRA Account

Company Contact Phone Number

Account No. Document Location URL

User Name Password Amount $

Company Retirement Plan

Company Contact Phone Number

Account No. Document Location URL

User Name Password Amount $

Corporate Business Interest

Company Contact Phone Number

Account No. Document Location URL

User Name Password Amount $

Real Estate

Description Owner

Address

Mortgage Bank Account No. FMV $

Life Insurance/Annuity

Company Contact Phone Number

Policy No. Document Location URL

User Name Password

Face Value $ Cash Value$

Life Insurance/Annuity

Company Contact Phone Number

Policy No. Document Location URL

User Name Password

Face Value $ Cash Value$

Insurance Agent

Name Company Phone Number

Email Address

User Name Password

Financial Advisor

Name Company Phone Number

Email Address

User Name Password

Attorney

Name Company Phone Number

Email Address

User Name Password

Estate Planning Documents

Will Y N

Trust Y N

Power of Attorney Y N

Health Care Proxy Y N

Chapter 9 | Immediate Needs

You and your attorney may decide that it is strategically advantageous to begin your home care application with an expedited program called the Immediate Needs program if the need for care is urgent and your loved one meets certain criteria.

Once the NYIA assessments and the Immediate Needs assessment are complete and you have been approved for Medicaid home care services, the care is then put in place by the local Medicaid field office. This is done directly through the LDSS and the care is paid for on under the fee-for-service paradigm. This expedited approach not only gets care in place faster, but also tends to result in getting more care hours approved than when applying directly into the Managed Long Term Care (MLTC) system because the care is paid for directly through Medicaid and not a managed care plan. MLTCs are paid a fixed number of dollars per patient per month, regardless of how many hours of care are given - thus, their incentive is to give as few hours as possible.

However, everyone is eventually transitioned from Immediate Needs to MLTC. At that point, the MLTC must maintain the number of hours authorized by Immediate Needs for 90 days after enrolling in the MLTC, regardless of the amount of hours and level of care. After the 90-day period, the MLTC can reassess the care given and attempt to decrease the number of hours. Because of this, strategically, it's better to start with Immediate Needs whenever possible.

On the other hand, when applying for Medicaid home care through an MLTC directly, there are several drawbacks. First, it often takes much longer to receive approval due to backlogs or other factors outside of our control. Second, the initial award of hours by the MLTC is not appealable, and this can result in fewer hours awarded than what is needed. Finally, the financial disincentive to give sufficient hours under the managed care paradigm. As such, it's important to be aware that if you choose to apply directly to an MLTC system instead of an Immediate Needs program, you may end up with fewer hours than what is needed.

In either instance, the same assessments will still need to take place, and the applicant will ultimately be transitioned into the regular home care program. However, by processing the initial application through Immediate Needs, the care will be in place so that the consumer is safe while the other steps are being done. The consumer will get the best and fastest hours from the inception, so there is much less chance of struggling to get the right number of hours in place.

I am inundated with calls from Medicaid recipients seeking appeals because they entered the system through the "wrong door," and are not able to get the hours necessary to keep them or their loved one safe.

I often find myself telling a prospective client that I wish they had known to reach out to me at the beginning of the process instead of mid-stream. There are a lot of different ways that people get into the home care system. Some people reach out to a care agency, and the agency brings them into one of the MLTCs that they contract with. Some people get referred directly to an MLTC from the discharge planner at the rehab or nursing home. Some people use various services that are out there to prepare their application. Some people start out with a pooled trust and then back into the application with the pooled trust's guidance. Still others file the application themselves. And then some people use an elder law attorney to assist. (You can probably guess which way I recommend.)

The way a person approaches the process will often determine the outcome. It will likely affect how quickly the care is put in place and how many hours are given.

I personally like to approach the process strategically.

If the client fits into the parameters of the Immediate Needs program, I will typically start there. The reason is this: If we start with the MLTC, it will take much longer, and we will get fewer hours. Full stop. No matter how much care a person needs, the MLTCs will usually offer 6 hours – AND – the initial award of hours by the MLTC is not appealable. This starts us out behind the 8 ball, and getting the hours the person really needs will be an uphill climb and will take considerable time and money.

Case Study

Jan (not her real name) called me in a state of desperation. Her mom had severe dementia and could not care for herself at all. Jan did everything she was told to do. She filed a Medicaid application. She attended the independent assessments through NYIA. Shortly thereafter, she received a letter from NYIA, stating her mom is eligible to receive care at home. The letter then said: "What happens next: Call us to learn about services". So, naturally, Jan immediately called the number, and NYIA gave her a list of MLTCs to choose from. She then called an MLTC and was told that it looked like her mom would only be able to receive four hours/day!

What was especially odd about this case was that Jan had applied through the Immediate Needs program (which most people don't even know about), so she should not have even been referred to an MLTC. She should have received an immediate call from the Home Care division of the local Medicaid office and been evaluated by them. Care should then have been put in place right away.

What did Jan do wrong? Absolutely nothing. She was given the wrong information by the state. Luckily, Jan could afford to hire counsel. What keeps me up at night is: What happens to the person who can't?

Case Study

Unlike Jan in the previous case study, Robert's dad had entered the system directly through MLTC.

Robert's father was wheelchair-bound and incontinent. He required assistance with all of his ADLs, but he was only given an aide for seven hours/day by the MLTC. He was told that's all he can get.

Because his father did not have the resources to privately pay for extra care, Robert had to go to his house after work every day and stay with his dad until the aide returned the next morning. Since his father had to go to the bathroom during the nighttime, Robert did not ever get a proper night's sleep. He had informed the MLTC of this, but they advised him that his father wasn't eligible for more hours because Robert was available as an "informal family support." (Robert didn't know that he did not have to agree to that.)

The Life Cycle of a Home Care Case

They don't make this process easy. By "they," I mean the multi-legged octopus that is Medicaid and the various branches of hierarchy overseeing it. It doesn't help that Medicaid is a state and federal program - that doesn't reduce the red tape. And the fact that downstream of the state bureaucracy are the local departments of social services run by the counties. And the county departments of social services have vendor agencies that they outsource the provision of care to. And then there are the MLTCs. And then there are the waivered programs that have their own overseers.

See what I mean?

Having worked with these programs for almost three decades, and having seen many changes over the years, I've learned that it's necessary to be very strategic in how we apply, what stages a case goes through, who handles what thing the best (hint: it's not always me!), what to do when the train falls off the tracks, who to beg for help, when to make complaints and when to appeal.

So, let's take a typical case.

1. The first step in a home care case is to make sure our client is eligible asset-wise. If we need to do estate planning and get assets out of their name, we must do that first.

2. The next step is to get the client eligible income-wise. There is one way to do that, and that is to join them to a pooled income trust, which was explained above in Chapter Five.

3. Then, we determine through which door we are going to enter the system. If our client meets the criteria for Immediate Needs, this is the door we choose. This is an expedited process that we do

directly through the Local Department of Social Services. This allows us to get certain really important things:

A. We get the care fast.

B. We're outside of the managed care paradigm, so we get the amount of care our client actually needs (meaning we aren't dealing with a private insurance plan whose primary goal is to spend as little as possible on each client).

C. The client gets "transition rights". What that means is once the client has been receiving services for several months, the state will tell them it's time for them to transition into MLTC (the managed care paradigm). However, unlike the client who applied directly into MLTC and got, e.g., six hours/day, the MLTC plan is required to keep the same care in place that the client is getting under the Immediate Needs program (which might be 24 hours, for instance) for 90 days. After that, if the MLTC reduces hours, the client can appeal. This is called "transition rights", and you want these.

4. Once we've decided to enter the system through the Immediate Needs door, the next step is to have the client schedule a fresh doctor's appointment. Immediately after the appointment, we reach out to the doctor's office to get the necessary medical forms and records.

5. As we're taking care of these items, the client has a checklist of needed documentation to find and forms to sign so we can put together the application.

6. When everything is ready, we file the application with all the required documents, the Immediate Needs forms, and the pooled trust documentation via e-fax. When Medicaid receives the application, they then separate the various parts: they send the application to the Eligibility Unit to determine eligibility; they send the medical form to the Home Care Unit to schedule the two state assessments and then they do their own assessment to determine how much care is needed; and they send the pooled trust approval request for initial review and then transmit it to the Department of Health. (Some counties are authorized to do these reviews on behalf of DOH. That is not the case with the New York City counties at this time.) This initial dissemination of the various parts of the application happens very quickly. Each of the units has different time frames within which their part must be completed. This makes the process very interesting to monitor.

Typically, when you come in through this door, you are very likely to be awarded high hours and keep them. It is not unusual for our clients to get round-the-clock care. Of course, this depends on their needs.

This is an example of a strategic approach to getting the right care in place from the beginning…

Immediate Needs Criteria

In order to be considered a consumer with an Immediate Need for Home Care Services, the consumer must meet the following conditions:

a. Have an immediate need for Personal Care or Consumer Directed Personal Assistance Services;

b. Have no informal caregivers available, able or willing to provide personal care services;

c. Have no home care agency providing needed assistance;

d. Does not have third-party insurance or Medicare benefits available to pay for needed assistance;

e. Does not have adaptive or specialized equipment or supplies in use to meet, or has adaptive or specialized equipment or supplies that cannot meet the person's need for assistance.

SAMPLE FORMS

MEDICAID APPLICATION CHECKLIST

IDENTITY AND BIRTHDATE

_____Birth or Baptismal Certificate (Applicant and Spouse)

_____Social Security Card (Applicant and Spouse)

_____Medicare Cards (Applicant and Spouse)

_____VA Discharge papers (Applicant and Spouse)

_____ ID

FAMILY RELATIONSHIPS

_____Marriage License

_____Divorce or Separation Agreement(s), if applicable

_____Death Certificate of Spouse, if applicable

RESIDENCE

_____Letters of Residence from 2 non-relatives

_____Real Estate Tax Bills

INCOME

_____Social Security Benefits Letter (Applicant and Spouse)

_____Pension Statement showing monthly gross and net amounts and all deductions (Applicant and Spouse)

_____Verification of any additional source of income i.e. IRA/Annuity distributions (Applicant and Spouse)

ASSETS AND RESOURCES

_____Stock Certificates and current value

_____Bonds (copy of each)

_____Insurance Policies (copy of policy and letter from company listing cash value of each policy)

_____Mortgage Agreements

_____Property Deeds

_____Checking account statements from _____ to current (opened and closed accounts)

_____Bankbooks and monthly statements from all Savings, Money Market, Annuity, IRA and other retirement and financial accounts from ____________ to current (opened and closed accounts)

_____Automobile Registration

OTHER

_____Supplemental Health Insurance Card (front and back) and current premium notice, i.e. Medicare, AARP

_____Prescription Drug Plan Card (front and back) and current premium notice

_____Income Tax Return for ____

_____HIPAA Release

Health Insurance Application - Department of Health – NYS

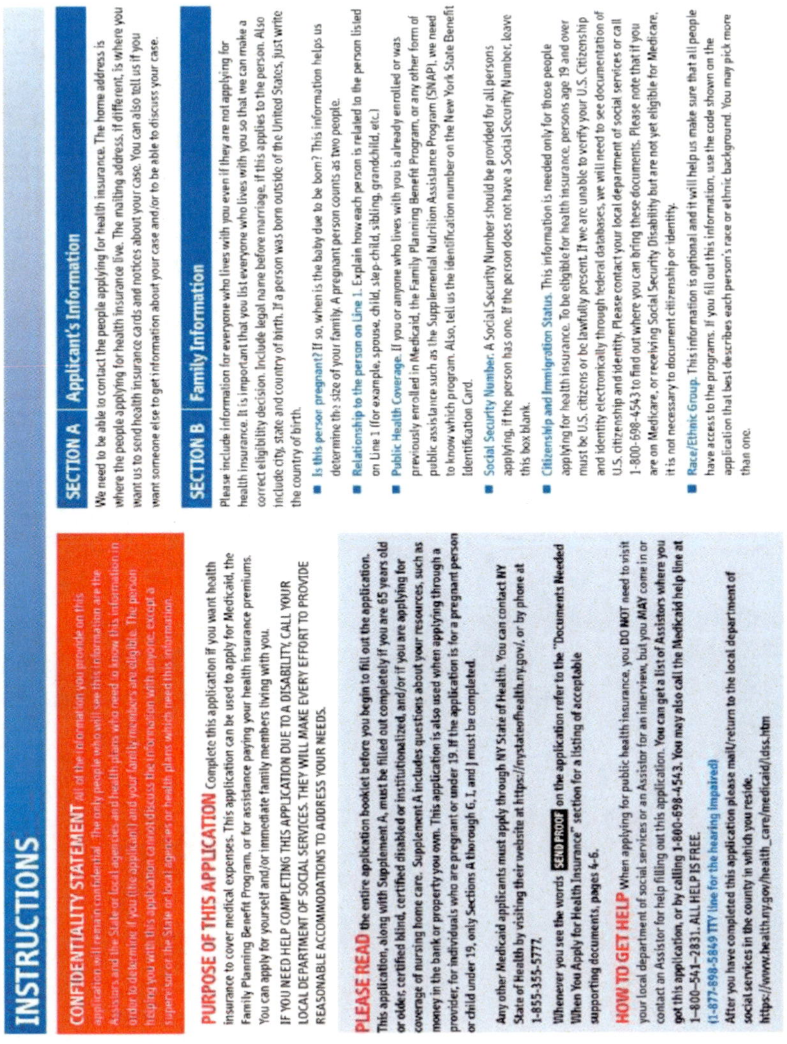

INSTRUCTIONS

CONFIDENTIALITY STATEMENT All of the information you provide on this application will remain confidential. The only people who will see this information are the Assisors and the State or local agencies and health plans who need to know this information in order to determine if you (the applicant) and your family members are eligible. The person helping you with this application cannot discuss the information with anyone, except a supervisor or the State or local agencies or health plans which need this information.

PURPOSE OF THIS APPLICATION Complete this application if you want health insurance to cover medical expenses. This application can be used to apply for Medicaid, the Family Planning Benefit Program, or for assistance paying your health insurance premiums. You can apply for yourself and/or immediate family members living with you.

IF YOU NEED HELP COMPLETING THIS APPLICATION DUE TO A DISABILITY, CALL YOUR LOCAL DEPARTMENT OF SOCIAL SERVICES. THEY WILL MAKE EVERY EFFORT TO PROVIDE REASONABLE ACCOMMODATIONS TO ADDRESS YOUR NEEDS.

PLEASE READ the entire application booklet before you begin to fill out the application. This application, along with Supplement A, must be filled out completely if you are 65 years old or older, certified blind, certified disabled or institutionalized, and/or if you are applying for coverage of nursing home care. Supplement A includes questions about your resources, such as money in the bank or property you own. This application is also used when applying through a provider, for individuals who are pregnant or under 19. If the application is for a pregnant person or child under 19, only Sections A thorough G, I, and J must be completed.

Any other Medicaid applicants must apply through NY State of Health. You can contact NY State of Health by visiting their website at https://nystateofhealth.ny.gov/, or by phone at 1-855-355-5777.

Whenever you see the words SEND PROOF on the application refer to the "Documents Needed When You Apply for Health Insurance" section for a listing of acceptable supporting documents, pages 4-6.

HOW TO GET HELP When applying for public health insurance, you **DO NOT** need to visit your local department of social services or an Assistor for an interview, but you **MAY** come in or contact an Assistor for help filling out this application. **You can get a list of Assistors where you got this application, or by calling 1-800-698-4543. You may also call the Medicaid help line at** 1–800–541–2831. ALL HELP IS FREE.
(1-877-898-5849 TTY line for the hearing impaired)
After you have completed this application please mail/return to the local department of social services in the county in which you reside.
https://www.health.ny.gov/health_care/medicaid/ldss.htm

SECTION A | Applicant's Information

We need to be able to contact the people applying for health insurance. The home address is where the people applying for health insurance live. The mailing address, if different, is where you want us to send health insurance cards and notices about your case. You can also tell us if you want someone else to get information about your case and/or to be able to discuss your case.

SECTION B | Family Information

Please include information for everyone who lives with you even if they are not applying for health insurance. It is important that you list everyone who lives with you so that we can make a correct eligibility decision. Include legal name before marriage, if this applies to the person. Also include city, state and country of birth. If a person was born outside of the United States, just write the country of birth.

- **Is this person pregnant?** If so, when is the baby due to be born? This information helps us determine the size of your family. A pregnant person counts as two people.
- **Relationship to the person on Line 1.** Explain how each person is related to the person listed on Line 1 (for example, spouse, child, step-child, sibling, grandchild, etc.)
- **Public Health Coverage.** If you or anyone who lives with you is already enrolled or was previously enrolled in Medicaid, the Family Planning Benefit Program, or any other form of public assistance such as the Supplemental Nutrition Assistance Program (SNAP), we need to know which program. Also, tell us the identification number on the New York State Benefit Identification Card.
- **Social Security Number.** A Social Security Number should be provided for all persons applying, if the person has one. If the person does not have a Social Security Number, leave this box blank.
- **Citizenship and Immigration Status.** This information is needed only for those people applying for health insurance. To be eligible for health insurance, persons age 19 and over must be U.S. citizens or be lawfully present. If we are unable to verify your U.S. Citizenship and identity electronically through federal databases, we will need to see documentation of U.S. citizenship and identity. Please contact your local department of social services or call 1-800-698-4543 to find out where you can bring these documents. Please note that if you are on Medicare, or receiving Social Security Disability but are not yet eligible for Medicare, it is not necessary to document citizenship or identity.
- **Race/Ethnic Group.** This information is optional and it will help us make sure that all people have access to the programs. If you fill out this information, use the code shown on the application that best describes each person's race or ethnic background. You may pick more than one.

DOH-4220 (11/23) page 1

SECTION C | Family Income (Money Received)

- In this section, list all types of income (money received) and the amounts received by the people you listed in Section B.
- Please tell us how much you make before taxes are taken out.
- If there is no money coming into your home, explain how you are paying for your living expenses, such as food and housing.
- We need to know if you have changed jobs or if you are a student.
- We also need to know if you pay another person or place, such as a day care center, to take care of your children or disabled spouse or parent while you are working or going to school. If you do, we need to know how much you pay. We may be able to deduct some of the amount that you pay for these costs from the amount we count as your income.

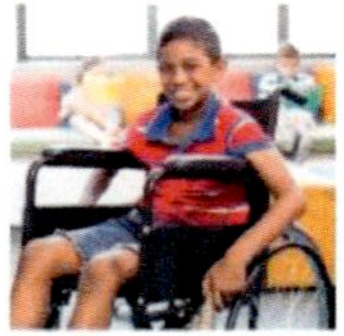

SECTION D | Health Insurance

It is important to tell us whether anyone applying is covered or could be covered by someone else's health insurance. For some applicants, we can deduct the amount that you pay for health insurance from the amount we count as your income; or we may be able to pay the cost of your health insurance premium if we determine it is cost effective. We may be able to help pay for health insurance premiums if you have or can get insurance through your job. We will need to gather more information about the insurance and will mail an insurance questionnaire to you.

If you are turning 65 within the next three months or you are 65 years of age or older, you may be entitled to additional medical benefits through the Medicare program. You are required to apply for Medicare as a condition of eligibility for Medicaid. Medicare is a federal health insurance program for people who are 65 or older and for certain people with disabilities regardless of income. When a person has both Medicare and Medicaid, Medicare pays first and Medicaid pays second. You are required to apply for Medicare if:

- You have Chronic Renal Failure (End Stage Renal Disease/ESRD) or Amyotrophic Lateral Sclerosis (ALS); OR
- You are turning 65 in the next three months or are already age 65 or older AND your income is at or below the Medicaid income level (based on the family size for a single individual or married couple). If so, then the Medicaid program can pay your premium or reimburse your Medicare premiums. If the Medicaid program can pay or reimburse your premiums, you will be required to apply for Medicare as a condition of Medicaid eligibility. Only citizens and lawful permanent residents who have lived in the U.S. continuously for five years must apply for Medicare. Many immigrants and non-citizens are not required to apply for Medicare.

SECTION E | Housing Expenses

Write in your monthly cost of housing. This includes your rent, monthly mortgage payment or other housing payment. If you have a mortgage payment, include property taxes in the mortgage amount you tell us. If you share your housing expenses or your rent is subsidized, please only tell us how much YOU pay toward your rent or mortgage. If you pay for your water, tell us how much you pay and how often.

SECTION F | Blind, Disabled, Chronically Ill or Nursing Home Care

These questions help us determine which program is best for each applicant, and what services may be needed. A person with a disability, serious illness or high medical bills may be able to get more health services. You may have a disability if your daily activities are limited because of an illness or condition that has lasted or is expected to last for at least 12 months. If you are blind, disabled, chronically ill or need nursing home care, you will need to complete Supplement A. If neither you nor anyone applying is blind, disabled, chronically ill or in a nursing home, go to Section G.

SECTION G | Additional Health Questions

If you have paid or unpaid medical bills from the past three months, Medicaid may be able to pay for these costs. Let us know who these bills are for and in which months the bills were incurred. Include copies of the medical bills with this application. Note: This three-month period begins when the local department of social services receives your application or when you meet with an Assistor to apply. You will need to tell us what your income was for any past months in which you have medical bills so that we can see if you are eligible during that time. We also ask about where you lived in the past three months, because this may affect our ability to pay for past bills. We ask about any pending lawsuits or health issues caused by someone else so we know if someone else should pay for any portion of your medical care costs.

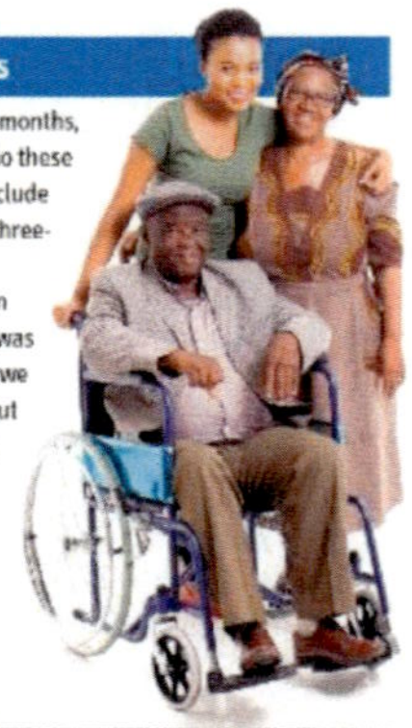

DOH-4220I (1/23) page 2

SECTION H | Parent or Spouse Not Living with the Family or Deceased

- **If any applicants have an absent spouse or parent, you must complete this section so we can see if medical support is available to you or your child.**
- **If you are pregnant, you do not have to answer these questions until 60 days after the birth of your child.** All other people who are applying and are age 21 or over must be willing to provide information about a parent of an applying minor or a spouse living outside the home to be eligible for health insurance, unless there is good cause. An example of "good cause" is fear of physical or emotional harm to you or a family member. Question 2 refers to the **PARENT** of any applying child under age 21. Question 3 refers to the **SPOUSE** of anyone applying.
- **If the applying parent** is not willing to provide this information, the applying child may still be eligible for Medicaid.

SECTION I | Health Plan Selection

What is a Health Plan? If you are found eligible for Medicaid, you may be required to get your health care coverage through a Managed Care health plan. A Managed Care health plan will provide your care by working with a network of doctors, clinics, hospitals and pharmacies to provide its members with high quality health care. When you join a plan, you choose one doctor (Primary Care Provider or PCP) from that plan to take care of your regular health and medical needs. If you want to keep the doctor you have, you need to pick a plan that works with your doctor. Managed Care health plans focus on preventive care so that small problems do not become big ones. If you need a specialist, your PCP can refer you to one in your plan's network.

Who Must Choose a Health Plan? MOST people who are eligible for Medicaid **MUST** choose a health plan to get most of their Medicaid benefits. Keep reading to find out how to get more information on this.

How Do I Know What Health Plan to Choose and If I Can Enroll?
For Medicaid, if you want to find out more about how managed care plans work, if you have to join, and how to choose a plan, call **Medicaid CHOICE** at **1-800-505-5678**, or call or visit your local department of social services. Ask for a Managed Care Education Packet. Information about health plans is also on the NYS Department of Health website at **www.health.ny.gov**. You can also enroll by phone, by calling **1-800-505-5678**.

NOTE: If you or a family member are found eligible for Medicaid, and are an American Indian/Alaska Native you are not required to join a health plan. You **will** still be enrolled in the health plan you choose, unless you check the box on the application that says you don't want to be enrolled, or tell us you do not want to be enrolled by calling or writing to your local department of social services.

SECTION J | Signature

Please read the paragraph in this section carefully and read the **Terms, Rights and Responsibilities** section. You must then sign and date the application. Remember to send the application to the local department of social services in the county in which you reside.

DOH-4220I (1/23) page 3

DOCUMENTS NEEDED WHEN YOU APPLY FOR HEALTH INSURANCE

Applicant Name **Application Date**

*** Your enrollment cannot be completed until all NECESSARY items are received.** *If you need help getting any of these items, let us know.*
YOU DO NOT NEED TO SHOW US **ALL** OF THESE DOCUMENTS. We only need documents that apply to you or others who are applying. If we are unable to verify your U.S. Citizenship and identity electronically through federal databases, we will need to see documentation of U.S. Citizenship and identity. Please do not mail original U.S. Citizenship or identity documents. Copies of other documents needed to determine eligibility can be mailed with your application or dropped off at your local department of social services. Please contact your local department of social services or call 1-800-698-4543 to find out where you can bring documents.

You need to provide proof of Identity, U.S. Citizenship and/or Immigration Status and Date of Birth.

You can provide ONE of the following documents to prove both U.S. Citizenship, Identity and your Date of Birth:

- ☐ U.S. passport/card
- ☐ Certificate of Naturalization (DHS Forms N-550 or N-570)
- ☐ Certificate of U.S Citizenship (DHS Forms N-560 or N-561)
- ☐ NYS Enhanced Driver's License (EDL).
- ☐ Native American Tribal Document issued by a Federally Recognized Tribe

When none of the above documents are available, ONE document from the U.S. Citizenship list and ONE from the Identity list may be used to prove your citizenship and /or identity.
This list is not all-inclusive. If you do not have one of these documents, please refer to the "How to Get Help" section of the instructions.

Documents with * next to it also show date of birth

U.S. Citizenship (Provide One)

- ☐ U.S. Birth Certificate*
- ☐ Certification of Birth issued by Department of State (Forms FS-545 or DS-1350)*
- ☐ Report of Birth Abroad (FS-240)
- ☐ U.S. National ID card (Form I-197 or I-179)
- ☐ Religious/School Records*
- ☐ Military record of service showing U.S. place of birth
- ☐ Final adoption decree
- ☐ Evidence of qualifying for U.S. citizenship under the Child Citizenship Act of 2000

AND

Identity (Provide One)

- ☐ State Driver's license or ID card with photo*
- ☐ ID card issued by a federal, state, or local government agency
- ☐ U.S. Military card or draft record or U.S Coast Guard Merchant Mariner Card
- ☐ School ID card with a photo (may also show date of birth)
- ☐ Certificate of Degree of Indian blood or other American Indian/Alaska Native tribal document with photo
- ☐ Verified School, Nursery or Daycare records (for children under 18) (may also show date of birth)
- ☐ Clinic, Doctor or Hospital records (for children under 18)*

If you do not have one of the documents that show your date of birth, you must also submit one of the following items:

- ☐ Marriage certificate
- ☐ NYS Benefit Identification Card

***Please return all necessary documents by: ____________________ or application may be denied.**

DOH-4220I (1/23) page 4

DOCUMENTS NEEDED WHEN YOU APPLY FOR HEALTH INSURANCE

If you are not a U.S. Citizen

The list below contains some of the most common United States Citizenship and Immigration Services (USCIS) forms used to show your immigration status.
This list is not all-inclusive. If you do not have one of these documents, please refer to the "How to Get Help" section of the instructions.

We need to see **ONE** of the following documents to prove Immigration Status, Identity and your Date of Birth. You must prove all three.
Documents with * next to it also show date of birth

Immigration Status/Identity

- ☐ I-551 Permanent Resident Card ("Green Card")*
- ☐ I-688B or I-766 Employment Authorization Card*

Immigration Status, but require an additional Identity document

- ☐ I-94 Arrival/Departure Record*
- ☐ USCIS Form I-797 Notice of Action

DOB/Identity, but require an additional immigration status document

- ☐ Visa
- ☐ U.S. Passport

Home Address: This address must match the home address that you write in Section A of the application. The proof must be dated within 6 months of when you signed the application.

- ☐ Lease/ letter/ rent receipt with your home address from landlord
- ☐ Utility Bill (gas, electric, phone, cable, fuel or water)
- ☐ Property tax records or mortgage statement
- ☐ Driver's license (if issued in the past 6 months)
- ☐ Government ID card with address
- ☐ Postmarked envelope or post card (cannot use if sent to a P.O. Box)

PROOF OF CURRENT INCOME, OR INCOME YOU MIGHT GET IN THE FUTURE SUCH AS UNEMPLOYMENT BENEFITS OR A LAWSUIT: You must provide a letter, written statement, or copy of check or stubs, from the employer, person or agency providing the income. YOU DO NOT NEED TO SHOW US ALL OF THESE DOCUMENTS, only the ones that apply to you and the people living with you.

One proof for each type of income you have is required. Provide the most recent proof of income before taxes and any other deductions. The proof must be dated, include the employee's name and show gross income for the pay period. The proof must be for the last four weeks, whether you get paid weekly, bi-weekly, or monthly. It is important that these be current.

Wages and Salary

- ☐ Paycheck stubs
- ☐ Letter from employer on company letterhead, signed and dated
- ☐ Business/payroll records

Self-Employment

- ☐ Current signed and dated income tax return and all Schedules
- ☐ Records of earnings and expenses/ business records

Unemployment Benefits

- ☐ Award letter/certificate
- ☐ Monthly benefit statement from NYS Department of Labor
- ☐ Printout of recipient's account information from the NYS Department of Labor's website (www.labor.ny.gov)
- ☐ Copy of Direct Payment Card with printout
- ☐ Correspondence from the NYS Department of Labor

Private Pensions/Annuities

- ☐ Statement from pension/annuity

Social Security

- ☐ Award letter/certificate
- ☐ Annual benefit statement
- ☐ Correspondence from Social Security Administration

Workers' Compensation

- ☐ Award letter
- ☐ Check stub

Child Support/Alimony

- ☐ Letter from person providing support
- ☐ Letter from court
- ☐ Child support/alimony check stub
- ☐ Copy of NY EPPICard with printout
- ☐ Copy of child support account information from **www.childsupport.ny.gov**
- ☐ Copy of bank statement showing direct deposit

Veterans' Benefits

- ☐ Award letter
- ☐ Benefit check stub
- ☐ Correspondence from Veterans Affairs

Military Pay

- ☐ Award letter
- ☐ Check stub

Income from Rent or Room/Board

- ☐ Letter from roomer, boarder, tenant
- ☐ Check stub

Interest/Dividends/Royalties

- ☐ Recent statement from bank, credit union or financial institution
- ☐ Letter from broker
- ☐ Letter from agent
- ☐ 1099 or tax return (if no other documentation is available)

DOH-4220f (1/23) page 5

DOCUMENTS NEEDED WHEN YOU APPLY FOR HEALTH INSURANCE

If you pay to have care for your children or an adult in your family while you work, provide one of the following:

- ☐ Written statement from day care center or other child/adult care provider
- ☐ Canceled checks or receipts that show your payments

If you or your spouse are required to pay court ordered support you must provide the following:

- ☐ Court Order

Proof of health insurance, provide all that apply:

- ☐ Proof of current insurance (Insurance policy, Certificate of Insurance or Insurance Card)
- ☐ Health Insurance Termination Letter
- ☐ Medicare Card (Red, White and Blue Card)
- ☐ Confirmation of Medicare Application
- ☐ Medicare Award or Denial Letter

If you have medical bills in the last three months, provide all the following (if applicable):

For determination of eligibility for medical expenses from the past three months:

- ☐ Proof of income for the month(s) in which the expense was incurred
- ☐ Proof of residency/home address for the month(s) in which the expense was incurred, if different from the address listed in Section A of this application
- ☐ Medical bills for last three months, whether or not you paid them

Resources (only if you are age 65 or older, certified blind or disabled and have no children under age 21 living with you):

- ☐ Bank account statements: checking, savings, retirement (IRA and Keogh)
- ☐ Stocks, bonds, certificates statements
- ☐ Copy of Life Insurance policy
- ☐ Copy of burial trust or fund burial plot deed or funeral agreement
- ☐ Deed for real estate other than residence

Proof of Student Status for college students if employed:

- ☐ Copy of schedule
- ☐ Statement from college or university
- ☐ Other correspondence from college showing student status

ACCESS NY HEALTH CARE Medicaid

Print clearly in blue or black ink. An incomplete application cannot be processed and will result in a delay of a decision on your application.

SECTION A | **Applicant's Information** Please tell us who you are and how to contact you.

Legal First Name		Middle Initial	Legal Last Name		
Primary Phone # ☐ Home ☐ Cell ☐ Work ☐ Other	Another Phone # ☐ Home ☐ Cell ☐ Work ☐ Other		What Language Do You: Speak? Read?		
HOME ADDRESS of the persons applying for health insurance **SEND PROOF** ☐ Check here if homeless	Street		Apt.#		
	City	State	Zip Code	County	
MAILING ADDRESS of the persons applying for health insurance if different from above.	Street		Apt.#		
	City		State	Zip Code	
OPTIONAL: If there is another person you would like to receive your Medicaid notices, please provide this person's contact information. I want this contact person to:	Name		State		
Check all that apply: ☐ Apply for and/or renew Medicaid for me ☐ Discuss my Medicaid application or case, if needed ☐ Get notices and correspondence	Street		Apt.#	Zip Code	
	City		Phone #		☐ Home ☐ Cell ☐ Work ☐ Other

Important Notice
Options Available to Applicants Who May Be Blind or Visually Impaired

If you are blind or visually impaired and require information in an alternative format, check the type of mail you want to receive from us.

☐ Standard notice and large print notice

☐ Standard notice and data CD notice

☐ Standard notice and audio CD notice

☐ Standard notice and braille notice, if you assert that none of the other alternative formats will be equally effective for you

If you require another accommodation, please contact your social services district.

APPLICATIONS FOR BENEFITS ADMINISTERED BY THE NEW YORK STATE MEDICAID PROGRAM (INCLUDING THE MEDICARE SAVINGS PROGRAM AND THE FAMILY PLANNING BENEFIT PROGRAM) ARE AVAILABLE IN LARGE PRINT AND DATA FORMATS. AUDIO AND BRAILLE VERSIONS OF THE APPLICATIONS ARE AVAILABLE FOR INFORMATIONAL PURPOSES ONLY.

DOH-4220 (1/23) page 1 of 10

SECTION B | **Family Information**

If you live in the household, start with yourself. If you do not, start with any adults who live in the household. List the full legal names of the persons applying for or already receiving Medicaid **and list the ID Number from their Benefit Card or health plan ID card.** You **must** provide information for family members including: parents, step-parents, and spouses. You may provide information for other family members (for example, a dependent child under the age of 21). **Listing other family members may allow us to give you a higher eligibility level. Applicants who are pregnant or under age 19 may be eligible for insurance regardless of immigration status.** New York State ensures your right to access State benefits and/or services regardless of your sex, gender identity, or expression. If you would like to provide us with how you or your household members currently identify, please also select gender identity.

		Date of Birth SEND PROOF / Sex	*Gender Identity (optional)	Is this person applying for health insurance?	Is this person pregnant?	Is this person the parent of an applying child?	What is the relationship to the person in Box 1?	If this person has or had public health coverage in the past, check the box that applies.	Social Security Number (If you have one)	Please mark one box that indicates your current Citizenship or Immigration Status. SEND PROOF	Race/ Ethnic Group (Optional)	**Received a service from the IHS, or other Indian Health Program?
1	Legal First, Middle, Last Name This person's birth name before they were married City State of Birth Country of Birth	__/__/____ ☐ Male ☐ Female ☐ X	☐ Male ☐ Female ☐ Non-Binary/ Non-Conforming ☐ X ☐ Transgender ☐ Different Identity Describe your identity (optional)	☐ Yes ☐ No	☐ Yes ☐ No What is the due date? __/__/__	☐ Yes ☐ No	SELF	☐ Child Health Plus ☐ Medicaid ☐ Family Health Plus ID Number from Benefit Card/Plan Card, if known:		☐ U.S. Citizen ☐ Immigrant/non-citizen Enter the date you received your immigration status __/__/____ MM DD YYYY ☐ Non-immigrant (Visa holder) ☐ None of the above	☐ B - Black or African American ☐ I - American Indian or Alaska Native ☐ W - White ☐ U - Unknown ☐ **A - Asian ☐ **P - Native Hawaiian or other Pacific Islander *Other AAPI Please also tell us if you are Hispanic or Latino ☐ H - Hispanic or Latino	☐ Yes ☐ No
2	Legal First, Middle, Last Name This person's birth name before they were married City State of Birth Country of Birth	__/__/____ ☐ Male ☐ Female ☐ X	☐ Male ☐ Female ☐ Non-Binary/ Non-Conforming ☐ X ☐ Transgender ☐ Different Identity Describe your identity (optional)	☐ Yes ☐ No	☐ Yes ☐ No What is the due date? __/__/__	☐ Yes ☐ No		☐ Child Health Plus ☐ Medicaid ☐ Family Health Plus ID Number from Benefit Card/Plan Card, if known:		☐ U.S. Citizen ☐ Immigrant/non-citizen Enter the date you received your immigration status __/__/____ MM DD YYYY ☐ Non-immigrant (Visa holder) ☐ None of the above	☐ B - Black or African American ☐ I - American Indian or Alaska Native ☐ W - White ☐ U - Unknown ☐ **A - Asian ☐ **P - Native Hawaiian or other Pacific Islander *Other AAPI Please also tell us if you are Hispanic or Latino ☐ H - Hispanic or Latino	☐ Yes ☐ No

SEND PROOF Refer to the "Documents Needed When You Apply for Health Insurance" on pages 4-6, for a list of documents that prove Identity, Citizenship or Immigration Status.

*Gender Identity: Gender identity is how you perceive yourself and what you call yourself. Your gender identity can be the same as or different from your sex.

**If you have selected A- Asian, or P- Native Hawaiian or Pacific Islander plese see below information on Other AAPI.

*Other Asian American/Pacific Islander (optional) - Please identify your AAPI subgroup. Subgroups within this community include, but are not limited to: Chinese, Japanese, Filipino, Korean, Vietnamese, Cambodian, Indonesian, Pakistani, Sri Lankan, Taiwanese, Native Hawaiian, Samoan, Tongan, Guamanian or Chamorro, Marshallese, Fijian, and other.

**Have you ever received a service from the Indian Health Service (IHS), a Tribal Health Program, an Urban Indian Health Program or through a referral from IHS or one of these programs?

DOH-4220 (1/23) page 2 of 10

SECTION B Family Information

Continued from previous page

#		Date of Birth SEND PROOF Sex	*Gender Identity (optional)	Is this person applying for health insurance?	Is this person pregnant?	Is this person the parent of an applying child?	What is the relationship to the person in Box 1?	If this person has or had public health coverage in the past, check the box that applies.	Social Security Number (if you have one)	Please mark one box that indicates your current Citizenship or Immigration Status. SEND PROOF	Race/ Ethnic Group (Optional)	**Received a service from the IHS, or other Indian Health Program?
3	Legal First, Middle, Last Name This person's birth name before they were married City State of Birth Country of Birth	__/__/____ ☐ Male ☐ Female ☐ X	☐ Male ☐ Female ☐ Non-Binary/ Non-Conforming ☐ X ☐ Transgender ☐ Different Identity Describe your identity (optional).	☐ Yes ☐ No	☐ Yes ☐ No What is the due date? __/__/__	☐ Yes ☐ No	SELF	☐ Child Health Plus ☐ Medicaid ☐ Family Health Plus ID Number from Benefit Card/Plan Card, if known:		☐ U.S. Citizen ☐ Immigrant/non-citizen Enter the date you received your immigration status __/__/____ MM DD YYYY ☐ Non-immigrant (Visa holder) ☐ None of the above	☐ B - Black or African American ☐ I - American Indian or Alaska Native ☐ W - White ☐ U - Unknown ☐ **A - Asian ☐ **P - Native Hawaiian or other Pacific Islander †Other AAPI Please identify if you are Hispanic or Latino ☐ H - Hispanic or Latino	☐ Yes ☐ No
4	Legal First, Middle, Last Name This person's birth name before they were married City State of Birth Country of Birth	__/__/____ ☐ Male ☐ Female ☐ X	☐ Male ☐ Female ☐ Non-Binary/ Non-Conforming ☐ X ☐ Transgender ☐ Different Identity Describe your identity (optional).	☐ Yes ☐ No	☐ Yes ☐ No What is the due date? __/__/__	☐ Yes ☐ No		☐ Child Health Plus ☐ Medicaid ☐ Family Health Plus ID Number from Benefit Card/Plan Card, if known:		☐ U.S. Citizen ☐ Immigrant/non-citizen Enter the date you received your immigration status __/__/____ MM DD YYYY ☐ Non-immigrant (Visa holder) ☐ None of the above	☐ B - Black or African American ☐ I - American Indian or Alaska Native ☐ W - White ☐ U - Unknown ☐ **A - Asian ☐ **P - Native Hawaiian or other Pacific Islander †Other AAPI Please identify if you are Hispanic or Latino ☐ H - Hispanic or Latino	☐ Yes ☐ No
5	Legal First, Middle, Last Name This person's birth name before they were married City State of Birth Country of Birth	__/__/____ ☐ Male ☐ Female ☐ X	☐ Male ☐ Female ☐ Non-Binary/ Non-Conforming ☐ X ☐ Transgender ☐ Different Identity Describe your identity (optional).	☐ Yes ☐ No	☐ Yes ☐ No What is the due date? __/__/__	☐ Yes ☐ No		☐ Child Health Plus ☐ Medicaid ☐ Family Health Plus ID Number from Benefit Card/Plan Card, if known:		☐ U.S. Citizen ☐ Immigrant/non-citizen Enter the date you received your immigration status __/__/____ MM DD YYYY ☐ Non-immigrant (Visa holder) ☐ None of the above	☐ B - Black or African American ☐ I - American Indian or Alaska Native ☐ W - White ☐ U - Unknown ☐ **A - Asian ☐ **P - Native Hawaiian or other Pacific Islander †Other AAPI Please identify if you are Hispanic or Latino ☐ H - Hispanic or Latino	☐ Yes ☐ No

Is anyone in your household a veteran? ☐ Yes ☐ No If yes, name: ____________

SEND PROOF Refer to the "Documents Needed When You Apply for Health Insurance" on pages 4-6, for a list of documents that prove Identity, Citizenship or Immigration Status.

*Gender Identity: Gender identity is how you perceive yourself and what you call yourself. Your gender identity can be the same as or different from your sex.

**If you have selected A- Asian, or P- Native Hawaiian or Pacific Islander plese see below information on Other AAPI.

†Other Asian American/Pacific Islander (optional) - Please identify your AAPI subgroup. Subgroups within this community include, but are not limited to: Chinese, Japanese, Filipino, Korean, Vietnamese, Cambodian, Indonesian, Pakistani, Sri Lankan, Taiwanese, Native Hawaiian, Samoan, Tongan, Guamanian or Chamorro, Marshallese, Fijian, and other.

**Have you ever received a service from the Indian Health Service (IHS), a Tribal Health Program, an Urban Indian Health Program or through a referral from IHS or one of these programs?

DOH-4220 (1/23) page 3 of 10

SECTION C | Family Income

Write the types of money and the amount received by everyone listed in Section B and **SEND PROOF**

Earnings from Work: Includes wages, salaries, commissions, tips, overtime, self-employment. If you are self-employed, check here: ☐ If no earnings from work, check here: ☐

Name of Person	Type of Income/Employer Name	How Much? (before taxes)	How Often? (weekly, monthly)

Unearned Income: Includes Social Security Benefits, disability payments, unemployment payments, interest and dividends, veterans' benefits, Workers' Compensation, child support payments/alimony, rental income, pension, annuities and trust income. If no unearned income, check here: ☐

Name of Person	Type of Income/Source	How Much? (before taxes)	How Often? (weekly, monthly)

Contributions: Money from relations or friends, roomers or boarders (include money that anyone gives you each month to help meet living expenses). If no contributions, check here: ☐

Name of Person	Type of Income/Source	How Much? (before taxes)	How Often? (weekly, monthly)

Other: Temporary (cash) Assistance, Supplemental Security Income (SSI) payments, student grants, or loans. If none, check here: ☐

Name of Person	Type of Income/Source	How Much? (before taxes)	How Often? (weekly, monthly)

If you or any applying adult in Section B does not have income, tell us who?

1. If there is no income listed above, please explain how you are living: (For example: living with friend or relative)
2. Have you or anyone who is applying changed jobs or stopped working in the last 3 months? ☐ No ☐ Yes
   If yes: Your last job was: Date / / Name of Employer:
3. Are you or anyone who is applying a student in a vocational, undergraduate, or graduate program? ☐ No ☐ Yes
   If yes: ☐ Full Time ☐ Part Time ☐ Undergraduate ☐ Graduate Name of Student:
4. Do you have to pay for childcare (or for the care of a disabled adult) in order to work or go to school? ☐ No ☐ Yes
   - Child's/Adult's Name: How Much? $ How Often? (weekly, every two weeks, monthly)
   - Child's/Adult's Name: How Much? $ How Often? (weekly, every two weeks, monthly)
   - Child's/Adult's Name: How Much? $ How Often? (weekly, every two weeks, monthly)
5. If you are not eligible for Medicaid coverage, you may still be eligible for the Family Planning Benefit Program. Are you interested in receiving coverage for Family Planning Services only? ☐ No ☐ Yes
6. Are you or your spouse / other parent required to pay court ordered support? ☐ No ☐ Yes Who How Much? $

DOH-4220 (1/23) page 4 of 10

SECTION D | Health Insurance

You and your family may still be eligible even if you have other health insurance.

1. Does anyone who is applying have Medicare? ☐ No ☐ Yes
   SEND PROOF
   If yes, include a copy of your card (red, white and blue card), for each Medicare beneficiary. Complete the rest of this application and complete Supplement A.
   If no, and you have Chronic Renal Failure (End Stage Renal Disease/ESRD) or Amyotrophic Lateral Sclerosis (ALS),or you are 65 years of age or older, or turning age 65 within three months, and do not have Medicare, you must apply for Medicare and show proof of application. Some people are required to apply for MEDICARE as a condition of eligibility for Medicaid. Please reference pages 2 and 3 (Section D) for additional information regarding eligibility requirements.

Note: If you are applying for the Medicare Savings Program (MSP) only, go to Section G. You do NOT need to complete Supplement A.

2. Does anyone who is applying already have other commercial health insurance, including long term care insurance? ☐ No ☐ Yes
   SEND PROOF
   If yes, you must send a copy of the front and back of the insurance card with this application.

Name of Insured (primary): ____ Persons Covered: ____

Cost of Policy: ____ End date of coverage, if ending soon ____ / ____ / ____ (Month / Day / Year)

3. Does your current job offer health insurance? ☐ No ☐ Yes
   We may be able to help pay for it.
   If yes, a "Request for Information Employer Sponsored Health Insurance" form will be sent to you.

SECTION E | Housing Expenses

1. Monthly housing payment such as rent or mortgage, including property taxes (just your share) $
2. If you pay for water separately how much do you pay? $ **SEND PROOF**

How often do you pay? ☐ every month ☐ 2 times a year ☐ quarterly (4 times a year) ☐ once a year

3. Do you receive free housing as part of your pay? ☐ No ☐ Yes

SECTION F | Blind, Disabled, Chronically Ill or Nursing Home Care

These questions help us determine which program is best for the applicants.

If no one is Blind, Disabled, Chronically Ill or in a Nursing Home STOP please go to Section G.

1. Are you, or anyone who lives with you and is applying, in a residential treatment facility or receiving nursing home care in a hospital, nursing home or other medical institution? ☐ No ☐ Yes
   If yes, finish completing this application AND complete Supplement A.
2. Are you or anyone who lives with you blind, disabled or chronically ill? ☐ No ☐ Yes
   If yes, finish completing this application AND complete Supplement A.

Note: If you are applying for the Medicare Savings Program only (MSP), go to Section G. You do not need to complete Supplement A.

DOH-4220 (1/23) page 5 of 10

SECTION G | Additional Health Questions

1. Does anyone applying have paid or unpaid medical or prescription bills for this month or the three months before this month? Medicaid may be able to pay these bills or reimburse you. ☐ No ☐ Yes If yes, name:
   In which month(s) of the previous three months do you have medical bills?

SEND PROOF **of income for any month in the three-month period for which you have bills. If you have paid medical bills for which you are seeking reimbursement, you must send copies and proof of payment.**

2. Do you, or anyone applying, have any unpaid medical or prescription bills older than the previous three months? ☐ No ☐ Yes
3. Have you, or anyone who lives with you and is applying, moved into this county from another state or New York State county within the past three months? ☐ No ☐ Yes If yes, who?
   Which state?
   Which county?
4. Does anyone who is applying have a pending lawsuit due to an injury? ☐ No ☐ Yes If yes, who?
5. Does anyone applying have a Workers' Compensation case or an injury, illness, or disability that was caused by someone else (that could be covered by insurance)? ☐ No ☐ Yes If yes, who?

SECTION H | Parent or Spouse Not Living with the Family or Deceased

Pregnant applicants and families who are applying only for their children are NOT required to fill out this section. All other people who are applying and are age 21 or over must be willing to provide information about a parent of an applying minor or a spouse living outside the home to be eligible for health insurance, unless there is good cause. Children may still be eligible even if a parent is not willing to provide this information. If you fear physical or emotional harm as a result of providing information about a parent or spouse not living in the home, you may be excused from providing this information. This is called **Good Cause.** You may be asked to show that you have a good reason for your fears.

1. Is the spouse or parent of anyone applying deceased? (If spouse or parent is deceased go to question 3.) ☐ No ☐ Yes If yes, name of applicant with deceased parent or spouse
2. Does a parent of any applying child live outside the home? (If no, skip to question 3) ☐ No ☐ Yes

If you fear physical or emotional harm if you provide information about a parent who does not live in the home, check this box ☐

Child's Name:	**Name of parent living outside the home**	**Current or last known address:**	
		Street:	City/State:
	Date of Birth (if known): / /	SSN (if known):	
Child's Name:	**Name of parent living outside the home**	**Current or last known address:**	
		Street:	City/State:
	Date of Birth (if known): / /	SSN (if known):	

3. Is anyone applying still married to someone who lives outside the home? ☐ No ☐ Yes If yes, name of person applying who is still married:

If you fear physical or emotional harm if you provide information about a spouse who does not live in the home, check this box ☐

Legal name of spouse living outside of the home:		**Current or last known address:**	
		Street:	City/State:
	Date of Birth (if known): / /	SSN (if known):	

DOH-4220 (1/23) page 6 of 10

SECTION I | Health Plan Selection

These questions help us determine which program is best for the applicants

If you are in receipt of Medicare, STOP skip this section.

IMPORTANT: Most people with Medicaid must choose a health plan; If you don't choose a health plan you may be automatically enrolled in one unless it is determined you are exempt. If you need information about what plans are available in your county, what plans your doctor is in and if you have to join, please call New York Medicaid CHOICE at 1-800-505-5678. You can also call or visit your local department of social services. If you already know what plan you want, use this section for your plan choice.

NOTE: If you or family members are found eligible for Medicaid, you will be enrolled in the health plan you choose. If you are an American Indian/Alaska Native you are not required to join a health plan; you can tell us you do not want to be in a health plan by calling or writing to your local department of social services or by checking this box ☐

Legal Last Name	Legal First Name	Date of Birth	Social Security #	Name of Health Plan You are Enrolling in	Preferred Doctor or Health Center (optional) Check Box If Your Current Provider	OB/GYN (optional)
					☐	
					☐	
					☐	
					☐	
					☐	
					☐	

SECTION J | Signature

I agree to have the information on this application and on the annual renewal shared only among Medicaid, the health plans indicated in Section I, the local department of social services, and the organization providing the application assistance. I also consent to sharing this information with any school-based health center that provides services to the applicant(s). I understand this information is being shared for the purpose of determining the eligibility of those individuals applying for Medicaid, or to evaluate the success of these programs. Each applying adult must sign this application in the space below.

I have read and understand the Terms, Rights and Responsibilities included in this application booklet on the next page. I certify under penalty of perjury that everything on this application is the truth as best I know.

Date | Signature of adult applicant or authorized representative for the applicant

Date | Signature of adult applicant or authorized representative for the applicant

Health Care Proxy

The New York Health Care Proxy Law allows you to choose someone you trust to make health care decisions for you if you can't make them for yourself. This person is called a health care agent. You can learn more about the New York State Health Care Proxy Law and get the form for a health care agent (proxy form) on the New York State Department of Health website at: www.health.ny.gov/professionals/patients/health_care_proxy

To get a copy of the form mailed to you, call the New York State Medicaid Help Line at 1-800-541-2831.

DOH-4220 (1/23) page 7 of 10

TERMS, RIGHTS AND RESPONSIBILITIES

By completing and signing this application, I am applying for Medicaid. I understand that this application and other supporting information will be sent to the program(s) for which I want to apply. I agree to the release of personal and financial information from this application and any other information needed to determine eligibility for these programs. I understand that I may be asked for more information. I agree to immediately report any changes to the information on this application.

- I understand that I must provide the information needed to prove my eligibility for each program. If I have been unable to get the information for Medicaid, I will tell the local department of social services. The local department of social services may be able to help in getting the information.
- If I am applying at a place other than a local department of social services, and my children are not found eligible for Medicaid using this application, I can contact the local department of social services to see if my children are eligible for Medicaid on some other basis.
- I understand that workers from the programs, for which family members or I have applied, may check the information given by me for this application. The agencies that run these programs will keep this information confidential according to 42 U.S.C. 1396a (a) (7) and 42 CFR 431.300-431.307, and any federal and state laws and regulations.
- I understand that Medicaid, will not pay medical expenses that insurance or another person is supposed to pay, and that if I am applying for Medicaid, I am giving to the agency all of my rights to pursue and receive medical support from a spouse or parents of persons under 21 years old and my right to pursue and receive third party payments for the entire time I am in receipt of benefits.
- I will file any claims for health or accident insurance benefits or any other resources to which I am entitled. I understand that I have the right to claim good cause not to cooperate in using health insurance if its use could cause harm to my health or safety or to the health and safety of someone I am legally responsible for.
- I understand that my eligibility for Medicaid will not be affected by my race, color, or national origin. I also understand that depending on the requirements of the program, my age, disability or citizenship status may be a factor in whether or not I am eligible.
- I understand that if my child is on Medicaid, they can get comprehensive primary and preventive care, including all necessary treatment through the Child/Teen Health Program. I can get more information on this program from the local department of social services.
- I understand that anyone who knowingly lies or hides the truth in order to receive services under these programs is committing a crime and subject to federal and state penalties and may have to repay the amount of benefits received and pay civil penalties. The New York State Department of Tax and Finance has the right to review income information on this form.

Social Security Number (SSNs)

SSNs are required for all applicants, unless the person is a non-qualified non-citizen. I understand that this is required by Federal Law at 42 U.S.C. 1320b-7 (a) and by Medicaid regulations at 42 CFR 435.910. SSNs are not required for members of my family who are not applying for benefits. If my eligibility depends on the amount of resources owned by my spouse, resources can be verified if my spouse's SSN is provided. SSNs are used in many ways, both within local department of social services (DSS) and between the DSS and federal, state, and local agencies, both in New York and other jurisdictions. Some uses of SSNs are: to check identity, to identify and verify earned and unearned income, to see if non-custodial parents can get health insurance coverage for their child(ren), to see if applicants can get medical support, to see if applicants can get money or other help, and to verify resources for applicants and their non-applying spouse. SSNs may also be used for identification of the recipient within and between central governmental Medicaid agencies to insure proper services are made available to the recipient.

For Medicaid Applicants Only

- Release of Educational Records
  I give permission to the local department of social services and New York State to obtain any information regarding the educational records of my child(ren), herein named, necessary for claiming Medicaid reimbursements for health-related educational services, and to provide the appropriate federal government agency access to this information for the sole purpose of audit.
- Early Intervention Program
  If my child is evaluated for or participates in the New York State Early Intervention Program, I give permission to the local department of social services and New York State to share my child's Medicaid eligibility information with my county Early Intervention Program for the purpose of billing Medicaid.
- Reimbursement of Medical Expenses
  I understand that I have a right as part of my Medicaid application, or later, to request reimbursement of expenses I paid for covered medical care, services and supplies received during the three month period prior to the month of my application. After the date of my application and ending on the date I receive my Medicaid benefit card (Common Benefit Identification Card (CBIC)), I understand that reimbursement of medically necessary covered medical care, services and supplies will **only** be available if obtained from Medicaid enrolled providers and that reimbursement is limited to no more than the Medicaid rate or fee in effect at the time of service, even if I paid more. I understand that once I receive my Medicaid (CBIC) benefit card, I must visit only Medicaid enrolled providers or network providers of my Medicaid managed care plan to obtain covered care and services, that my provider must submit a claim to Medicaid or my Medicaid managed care plan to be paid for medically necessary services and that no reimbursement will be made for expenses I incur after that date and pay for myself.

DOH-4220 (1/23) page 8 of 10

Medicaid Managed Care

I have read how to find out what Medicaid managed care health plans are available to me in my county. I understand that if I, and any members of my family who are applying, are found eligible for Medicaid and are required to be in a managed care health plan, I and any eligible family members who applied, will be enrolled in the health plan I choose.

I have read how to find out the rights and benefits that I will have as a member of a managed care health plan and the benefit limitations of managed care membership. I understand that in Medicaid managed care, I must choose a Primary Care Provider (PCP) and that I will have a choice from at least three PCPs in my health plan. I understand that once I enroll in a health plan, I will have to use my PCP and other providers in my health plan except in a few special circumstances.

I understand that if a child is born to me while I am a member of a Medicaid managed care health plan, my child will be enrolled in the same health plan that I am in.

Release of Medical Information

I consent to the release of any medical information about me and any members of my family for whom I can give consent:

- By my PCP, any other health care provider or the New York State Department of Health (NYSDOH) to my health plan and any health care providers involved in caring for me or my family, as reasonably necessary for my health plan or my providers to carry out treatment, payment, or health care operations. This may include pharmacy and other medical claims information needed to help manage my care;
- By my health plan and any health care providers to NYSDOH and other authorized federal, state, and local agencies for purposes of administration of the Medicaid programs; and
- By my health plan to other persons or organizations, as reasonably necessary for my health plan to carry out treatment, payment, or health care operations.

I also agree that the information released for treatment, payment and health care operations may include HIV, mental health or alcohol and substance abuse information about me and members of my family to the extent permitted by law, until I revoke this consent.

If more than one adult in the family is joining a Medicaid health plan, the signature of each adult applying is necessary for consent to release information.

Notice of Nondiscrimination Policy

The New York Medicaid program complies with applicable Federal civil rights laws and state laws and does not discriminate on the basis of race, color, national origin, creed/religion, sex, age, marital/family status, disability, arrest record, criminal conviction(s), gender identity, sexual orientation, predisposing genetic characteristics, military status, domestic violence victim status and/or retaliation.

If you believe that the New York Medicaid program has discriminated against you, you may file a complaint by going to: http://www.health.ny.gov/regulations/discrimination_complaints/ or, by emailing the Diversity Management Office at DMO@health.ny.gov.

You may also file a civil rights complaint with the U.S. Department of Health and Human Services, Office for Civil Rights electronically at: https://ocrportal.hhs.gov/ocr/portal/lobby.jsf or by mail or phone at U.S. Department of Health and Human Services, 200 Independence Avenue, SW, Room 509F, HHH Building, Washington, D.C. 20201; 800-368-1019 (TTY 800-537-7697). Complaint forms are available at https://www.hhs.gov/ocr/complaints/index.html.

Accommodations

The New York Medicaid program provides free aid and services to people with disabilities to communicate effectively with us,
such as:

- TTY through NY Relay Service
- If you are blind or seriously visually impaired and need notices or other written materials in an alternative format (large print, audio, or data CD, or Braille), and you reside in a county outside of New York City, please call your local department of social services. If you reside in the five boroughs of New York City, please call the Human Resources Administration's Office of Constituent Services at 212-331-4640. Or tell us in Section A on page 1 of this application.

The NY Medicaid Program also provides free language assistance services to people whose primary language is not English such as:

- Qualified interpreters
- Written information in other languages

If you need these services or for more information on Reasonable Accommodations, and you reside in a county outside of New York City, please call your local department of social services. If you reside in the five boroughs of New York City, please call the Human Resources Administration's Office of Constituent Services at 212-331-4640.

DOH-4220 (1/23) page 9 of 10

For Office Use Only

To be completed by the person assisting with the application

Signature of Person Who Obtained Eligibility Information:	Employed By: (check one) ☐ Health Plan ☐ Local Department of Social Services ☐ Provider Agency ☐ Qualified Entities
X	Employer Name:

To be used by the local social services district

Eligibility Determined By:		Date:	Eligibility Approved By:	Date:
Center Office:		Application Date:	Unit ID:	Worker ID:
Case Name:	District:	Case Type:		Case #:
Effective Date:	MA Disposition Reason Code ☐ Denial Code ☐ Withdrawal Code	Proxy: ☐ No ☐ Yes	Registry #:	Ver:

DOH-4220 (1/23) page 10 of 10

Department of Health

DOH-4220 (1/23)

Supplement to Access NY Health Care Application

Supplement A

(Supplement to Access NY Health Care Application DOH-4220)

This Supplement must be completed if anyone who is applying is:

- Age 65 or older
- Certified blind or certified disabled (of any age)
- Not certified disabled but chronically ill
- Institutionalized and applying for coverage of nursing home care. This includes care in a hospital that is equivalent to nursing home care.

Note: If you are applying for the Medicare Savings Program (MSP) only, this Supplement does not need to be completed.

INSTRUCTIONS:

- Sections A through E must be completed and this Supplement must be signed.
- If you or anyone in your household is applying for coverage of nursing home care, you must also complete sections F through G.

A. Applicant and Spouse Information

1. Applicant(s) this Supplement is being completed for:

Legal Last Name	Legal First Name	MI	Marital Status	Social Security Number	Date of Birth	If Deceased, List Date of Death
					/ /	/ /
					/ /	/ /

Is a person named above:

- Chronically ill? ☐ Yes ☐ No
  (Examples of chronically ill would be unable to work for at least 12 months because of an illness or injury, or having an illness or disabling impairment that has lasted or is expected to last for 12 months.)
- Certified Blind by the Commission for the Blind and Visually Handicapped? ☐ Yes ☐ No
  (If yes, send proof.)
- Interested in applying for the MBI-WPD program if disabled and working? ☐ Yes ☐ No
  The Medicaid Buy-In for Working People with Disabilities (MBI-WPD) program offers Medicaid coverage to people who are disabled, working, and at least 16 years old but not yet 65 years old. The program allows higher income levels than the regular Medicaid program so working people with disabilities can earn more and keep their Medicaid coverage.

DOH - 5178A 8/15 (page 1 of 8) NYS DOH

If an applicant is living in a long-term care facility/nursing home, adult home, or assisted living facility, provide the following information.

Name of Applicant who is in Facility	Name of Facility	Date Admitted / /	Telephone Number ( ) -
Street Address	City	State	Zip Code
Applicant's Previous Address	City	State	Zip Code

If the above previous address was also a facility or adult home, list the address prior to admission below.

Applicant's Second Previous Address	City	State	Zip Code

2. Applicant's Spouse: (if not listed above)

Legal Last Name		Legal First Name	MI
Maiden Name or Other Name Known By:		Social Security Number	Date of Birth / /
Street Address (if in a facility, list spouse's address prior to being admitted to facility)			
City	State		Zip Code

Is the applicant's spouse living in a long-term care facility/nursing home? ☐ Yes ☐ No

If **yes**, provide the following information:

Name of Facility		Date Admitted / /	Telephone Number ( ) -
Street Address	City	State	Zip Code

Is the applicant's spouse deceased? ☐ Yes ☐ No **If yes**, what is the date of death? ____/____ /____

DOH - 5178A 8/15 (page 2 of 8) NYS DOH

B. What Care and Services are you Applying for? (check the box that applies)

☐ **You are applying for Medicaid coverage but not coverage of community-based long-term care services.** You may attest to the amount of your resources. You are not required to submit documentation of your resources at this time. If a computer match shows something different than what you reported, you may be asked to submit proof at a later date.

This coverage does not include nursing home care, home care or any of the community-based long-term care services listed below.*

☐ **You are applying for coverage of community-based long-term care services.** Documentation of the **current** amount of your resources is required. However, you only need to submit documentation for certain resources at this time. See "Documentation Requirements" below for a list of these resources.

This coverage includes the following services:*

- Adult day health care
- Limited licensed home care
- Private duty nursing
- Hospice in the community
- Hospice residence program
- Assisted living program
- Consumer directed personal assistance program
- Certified Home Health Agency services
- Residential treatment facility care
- Personal emergency response services
- Personal care services
- Managed long-term care in the community
- Waiver and other services provided through a home and community-based waiver program

Note: Some examples of home and community-based programs that provide waiver and other services are Traumatic Brain Injury Program and Nursing Home Transition and Diversion Program.

☐ **You are institutionalized and applying for coverage of nursing home care.** Documentation of your resources for the **past 60 months** is required. However, you only need to submit documentation for certain resources at this time. See "Documentation Requirements" below for a list of these resources.

*You may be eligible for short-term rehabilitation services. Short-term rehabilitation services include one commencement/admission in a 12-month period of up to 29 consecutive days of nursing home care and/or certified home health care.

DOCUMENTATION REQUIREMENTS

If you are requesting coverage for **community-based long-term care services** or **nursing home care,** provide documentation for the time period indicated above for all of the following resources, if applicable.

- Life insurance policy;
- Securities, stocks, bonds, and mutual funds;
- Annuities;
- Burial agreement or fund;
- Trust document and accounts.

You do not need to send proof of any other resources at this time. This is because other resources may be verified through computer matches. If the resources you report do not match our records or cannot be verified through our records, we may ask you to submit proof of those other resources at a later date.

C. Resources/Assets

INSTRUCTIONS FOR SECTIONS 1 THROUGH 8:

- List all resources currently owned by you and/or your spouse/parent(s), including custodial accounts.
- Check the **"NONE"** box if you and/or your spouse/parent(s) do not own any of those resources.
- **If applying for coverage of nursing home care,** also list any accounts CLOSED in the **past 60 months;** include the balance at closing and provide an explanation of where the balance was transferred to or how it was spent. On a separate sheet of paper, provide an explanation of each transaction of $2,000 or more.
  Note: Medicaid retains the right to review all transactions made during the transfer look-back period.

1. Checking/Savings/Credit Union Accounts/Certificates of Deposits (CDs): ☐ **NONE**

Bank Name	Account Number	Name of Owner(s)	Current Account Balance	Closed Accounts: Date Closed	Closed Accounts: Balance at Closing
			$	/ /	$
			$	/ /	$
			$	/ /	$
			$	/ /	$
			$	/ /	$
			$	/ /	$
			$	/ /	$
			$	/ /	$
			$	/ /	$

2. Retirement Accounts (Deferred Compensation, IRA and/or Keogh): ☐ **NONE**

Institution Name	Account Number	Name of Owner(s)	Pay Out	Current Account Balance	Closed Accounts: Date Closed	Closed Accounts: Balance at Closing
			☐ Yes ☐ No	$	/ /	$
			☐ Yes ☐ No	$	/ /	$
			☐ Yes ☐ No	$	/ /	$
			☐ Yes ☐ No	$	/ /	$

3. Annuities, Stocks, Bonds, Mutual Funds: ☐ **NONE**

Institution/Company Name	Account Number	Name of Owner(s)	Date Purchased	Current Value	Closed Accounts: Date Closed or Sold	Closed Accounts: Value at Closing
				$	/ /	$
				$	/ /	$
				$	/ /	$
				$	/ /	$
				$	/ /	$
				$	/ /	$
				$	/ /	$

DOH - 5178A 8/15 (page 4 of 8) NYS DOH

4. Life Insurance Policies:						☐ **NONE**
					Cancelled Policies	
Insurance Company	Policy Number	Name of Owner(s)	Current Cash Value	Current Face Value	Date Cancelled	Cash Out Value
			$	$	/ /	$
			$	$	/ /	$
			$	$	/ /	$
			$	$	/ /	$
			$	$	/ /	$

5. Burial Assets/Burial Contracts: (Include copies): ☐ **NONE**

a. Do you and/or your spouse have a pre-paid funeral agreement for you or anyone else in your family? ☐ Yes ☐ No

b. Do you and/or your spouse have a burial space or plot for you or anyone else in your family? ☐ Yes ☐ No

c. Do you and/or your spouse have money in a bank account set aside for a burial fund? ☐ Yes ☐ No

If **yes**, in what account(s) is your and/or your spouse's burial fund?

Bank Name and Account Number	Name of Owner(s)	Value
		$
		$
		$

d. Do you have life insurance to be used as your burial fund? ☐ Yes ☐ No

If **yes**, what is your policy number(s)? ______________________

If **yes**, is the full cash value to be used for your burial expenses? ☐ Yes ☐ No

e. Does your spouse have life insurance to be used as a burial fund? ☐ Yes ☐ No

If **yes**, what is the policy number(s)? ______________________

If **yes**, is the full cash value to be used for burial expenses? ☐ Yes ☐ No

6. Trust Accounts: If you and/or your spouse created or are the beneficiary of a trust, submit a copy of the trust, including the current schedule of trust assets. ☐ **NONE**

Name of Trust	Grantor	Trustee(s)	Assets	Beneficiary	Income
			$		$
			$		$
			$		$
			$		$

7. Vehicle(s): List all cars, trucks and vans. List all recreational vehicles, including campers, snowmobiles, boats and motorcycles. ☐ **NONE**

Name of Owner(s)	Year/Make/Model	Fair Market Value	Amount Owed	In use?	Date Sold
			$	☐ Yes ☐ No	/ /
			$	☐ Yes ☐ No	/ /
			$	☐ Yes ☐ No	/ /

DOH - 5178A 8/15 (page 5 of 8) NYS DOH

8. List Any Other Resources:

Resource Type	Name of Owner(s)	Value
		$
		$
		$
		$
		$
		$

D. Homestead

1. Do you and/or your spouse own or have a legal interest in your home, including a life estate? ☐ Yes ☐ No
2. If you are in a medical facility and own your home, do you intend to return to your home? ☐ Yes ☐ No

   If **no**, is anyone living in the home? ☐ Yes ☐ No

   Who is living in the home? ____________________

   How is this person related to you and/or your spouse? ____________________

   If you and/or your spouse's child (of any age) is living in the home, is the child disabled? ☐ Yes ☐ No

   Note: If there is a legal impediment that prevents you from selling this property, the property is not counted in determining Medicaid eligibility. **Send proof of legal impediment.**

3. Equity Value in Home:
   If you own your home, what is the equity value in your home? $ ____________________
   Note: Equity value is the fair market value less any outstanding liens, mortgages, etc.

E. Real Property (other than your home)

Do you and/or your spouse own or have a legal interest in any other real property? (Check any that apply) ☐ Yes ☐ No

☐ Rental Property ☐ Vacation Property ☐ Time Share ☐ Vacant Land ☐ Other Property Rights (In or outside of New York State)

If **yes**, provide the following information:

Name and Address of Owner(s)	Address of Property	Type of Ownership (Check one)	Equity value
		☐ Individual ☐ Joint tenancy ☐ Life estate	$
		☐ Individual ☐ Joint tenancy ☐ Life estate	$
		☐ Individual ☐ Joint tenancy ☐ Life estate	$
		☐ Individual ☐ Joint tenancy ☐ Life estate	$

STOP HERE unless you or anyone in your household is institutionalized and applying for coverage of nursing home care. However, Section I of this document MUST be signed.

DOH - 5178A 8/15 (page 6 of 8) NYS DOH

F. Asset Transfers

1. Transfers

a. In the last 60 months, did you, your spouse, or someone on your behalf transfer, change ownership in, give away, or sell any assets, including your home or other real property? ☐ Yes ☐ No

b. In the last 60 months, have you or your spouse created or transferred any assets into or out of a trust? ☐ Yes ☐ No

If you answered yes to either of the questions above, explain the transfer(s) below. Attach additional sheets of paper, if needed.

Description of Asset (including income)	Date of Transfer	Transferred to Whom	Amount of Transfer
			$
			$
			$
			$

c. Are you in the process of selling property? ☐ Yes ☐ No

d. In the last 60 months, did you, your spouse or someone on your behalf, change the deed or the ownership of any real property, including creating a life estate? ☐ Yes ☐ No

If **yes**, when? ____________________

e. If you purchased a life estate in another person's home, did you live in the home for at least one year after you purchased the life estate? ☐ Yes ☐ No

f. In the last 60 months, did you, your spouse, or someone on your behalf purchase a mortgage, loan, or promissory note? ☐ Yes ☐ No

If **yes**, when? ____________________

g. In the last 60 months, did you, your spouse, or someone on your behalf purchase or change an annuity? ☐ Yes ☐ No

If **yes**, when? ____________________

2. Have you, your spouse, or someone acting on your behalf given a deposit to any health care or residential facility, such as a nursing home, assisted living facility, continuing care retirement community or life care community? ☐ Yes ☐ No

If yes, send copy of agreement.

G. Tax Returns

Did you and/or your spouse file U.S. income tax returns in the last four years? ☐ Yes ☐ No

If yes, send complete copies of these returns including all schedules and attachments.

DOH - 5178A 8/15 (page 7 of 8) NYS DOH

H. Important Information

Liens on Real Property

Upon receipt of Medicaid, a lien may be filed and a recovery may be made against your real property under certain circumstances if you are in a medical institution and not expected to return home. Medicaid paid on your behalf may be recovered from persons who had legal responsibility for your support at the time medical services were obtained. Medicaid may also recover the cost of services and premiums incorrectly paid.

Transfer of Assets

Federal and State laws provide that an individual may be found ineligible for nursing facility services for a period of time if an individual or an individual's spouse transfers an asset for less than fair market value within the look-back period. The look-back period is the 60 months immediately prior to the date an individual is both institutionalized and has applied for Medicaid.

Annuities

As a condition of Medicaid coverage for nursing facility services, applicants are required to disclose a description of any interest the individual or the individual's spouse has in an annuity. This disclosure is required regardless of whether the annuity is irrevocable or a countable resource.

In addition to the purchase of an annuity, certain transactions made to an annuity by the applicant or the applicant's spouse within the look-back period, may be treated as a transfer unless:

- The State is named the remainder beneficiary in the first position for at least the amount of Medicaid paid on behalf of the annuitant; or
- The State is named in the second position after a community spouse or minor or disabled child, or in the first position if such spouse or representative of such child disposes of any such remainder for less than fair market value.

If documentation is not submitted verifying that the State has been named remainder beneficiary, you may be ineligible for coverage of nursing facility services.

If the annuity is a countable resource at the time of application, you/your spouse are not required to name the State as remainder beneficiary.

I. Certification and Authorization

I certify under penalty of perjury, that the information on this form is correct and complete to the best of my knowledge. I understand that I must report any changes in this information within 10 days of the change.

If eligibility depends on the amount of my and my spouse's resources, by signing this application we authorize verification of our resources with financial institutions for the purpose of determining eligibility. Both spouses must sign below. This authorization will end if my application for Medicaid is denied, or I am no longer eligible for Medicaid, or I/we revoke this authorization in a written statement to my local Department of Social Services.

X ______________________________ X ______________________
SIGNATURE OF APPLICANT/REPRESENTATIVE DATE SIGNED

X ______________________________ X ______________________
SIGNATURE OF APPLICANT'S SPOUSE DATE SIGNED

DOH - 5178A 8/15 (page 8 of 8) NYS DOH

IMMEDIATE NEED TRANSMITTAL TO THE HOME CARE SERVICES PROGRAM

NYC Human Resources Administration, Department of Social Services

HCSP-3052 (E) 09/19/2016

DATE: ______ CONSUMER'S NAME: ______ LAST 4 DIGITS OF CONSUMER'S SSN: ______

From
NAME OF SUBMITTING ORGANIZATION
STREET ADDRESS
CITY, STATE, ZIP CODE

To:
HOME CARE SERVICES PROGRAM – IMMEDIATE NEEDS
785 ATLANTIC AVENUE, 7th Floor
BROOKLYN, NY 11238

I am submitting this application package on behalf of the above named consumer for processing as an "Immediate Need" for home care services. S/he wishes to be enrolled in the following program (check one):

☐ Personal Care (PCS) ☐ Consumer Directed Personal Assistance (CDPAS)

I understand that the documentation listed in the table(s) below is **required** for this request to be processed. All are attached and appear to be fully completed.

For **all** Immediate Need Requests

OHIP-0103, **Attestation of Immediate Need**	HCSP M-11q, **Medical Request for Home Care**	OCA-960, **Authorization for Release of Health Information Pursuant to HIPAA**

Also required, in addition to the three items listed above, **if the consumer already has Medicaid coverage, but it does not include long term care coverage**

DOH-4495A, **Access NY Supplement A**	All necessary proofs that apply to this supplemental form **only**, as detailed in the DOH-4220 **"Documents Needed When You Apply For Public Health Insurance"** section

Also, required in addition to everything listed in both tables above, **if the consumer does not already have Medicaid coverage at all**

DOH-4220, **Access NY Insurance Application**	All necessary proofs as detailed in the DOH-4220 **"Documents Needed When You Apply For Public Health Insurance"** section

Though not required, I understand that submission of a cover letter that includes an explanation of the immediate need, the status of consumer's current whereabouts, a listing of submitted documents, the type of service requested (PCS or CDPAS), is strongly recommended.

☐ I have attached a cover letter ☐ I have not submitted a cover letter

Print Name:	Sign Name:	Telephone Number:

NEW YORK STATE DEPARTMENT OF HEALTH
Division of Program Development and Management

Immediate Need for Personal Care/Consumer Directed Personal Assistance Services Informational Notice and Attestation Form

IMMEDIATE NEED FOR PERSONAL CARE SERVICES/CONSUMER DIRECTED PERSONAL ASSISTANCE SERVICES

If you think you have an immediate need for Personal Care Services (PCS) or Consumer Directed Personal Assistance Services (CDPAS), such as housekeeping, meal preparation, bathing, or toileting, your eligibility for these services may be processed more quickly if you meet the following conditions:

- You have no informal caregivers available, able and willing to provide or continue to provide care;
- You are not receiving needed help from a home care services agency;
- You have no adaptive or specialized equipment or supplies in use to meet your needs; and
- You have no third party insurance or Medicare benefits available to pay for needed help.

If you don't already have Medicaid coverage, and you meet the above conditions, you may ask to have your Medicaid application processed more quickly by sending in: a completed Access NY Health Insurance Application (DOH-4220); the Access NY Supplement A (DOH-5178A), if needed; a physician's order (DOH-4359 or HCSP-M11Q) or Practitioner Statement of Need (DOH-5779) for services (see NOTE below); and a signed "Attestation of Immediate Need" (page 3 of this notice).

If you already have Medicaid coverage that does not include coverage for community-based long term care services, you must send in a completed Access NY Supplement A (DOH-5178A); a physician's order (DOH-4359 or HCSP-M11Q) or Practitioner Statement of Need (DOH-5779) for services (see NOTE below); and a signed "Attestation of Immediate Need" (page 3 of this notice).

If you already have Medicaid coverage that includes coverage for community-based long term care services, you must send in a physician's order (DOH-4359 or HCSP-M11Q) or Practitioner Statement of Need (DOH-5779) for services (see NOTE below) and a signed "Attestation of Immediate Need" (page 3 of this notice).

NOTE: If you are under 18 years of age, you must have a physician's order form (DOH-4359 or HCSP-M11Q). If you are 18 or older, you can have either a Practitioner Statement of Need form (DOH-5779) or a physician's order (DOH-4359 or M11Q).

If you don't already have Medicaid coverage or you have Medicaid coverage that does not include coverage for community-based long term care services: All of the required forms (see the appropriate list, above) must be sent to your local social services office or, if you live in NYC, to the Human Resources Administration (HRA). As soon as possible after receiving all of these forms, the social services office/HRA will then check to make sure that you have sent in all the information necessary to determine your Medicaid eligibility. If more information is needed, they must send you a letter, no later than four days after receiving these required forms, to request the missing information. This letter will tell you what documents or information you need to send in and the date by which you must send it. By no later than 7 days after the social service office/HRA receives the necessary information, they must let you know if you are eligible for Medicaid. By no later than 12 days after receiving all the necessary information, the social services office/HRA will also determine whether you could get PCS or CDPAS if you are found eligible for Medicaid. You cannot get this home care from Medicaid unless you are found eligible for Medicaid. If you are found eligible for Medicaid and PCS or CDPAS, the social services office/HRA will let you know and you will get the home care as quickly as possible.

DOH-5786 (11/22) Page 1 of 3

If you already have Medicaid coverage that includes coverage for community-based long term care services:
The physician's order (DOH-4359 or HCSP-M11Q) or Practitioner Statement of Need (DOH-5779), and the signed Attestation of Immediate Need must be sent to your local social services office or HRA. By no later than 12 days after receiving these required forms, the social services office/HRA will determine whether you can get PCS or CDPAS. If you are found eligible for PCS or CDPAS, the social services official/HRA will let you know and you will get the home care as quickly as possible.

The necessary forms may be obtained from your local department of social services or are available to be printed from the Department of Health's website at: http://www.health.ny.gov/health_care/medicaid/#apply

NEW YORK STATE DEPARTMENT OF HEALTH
Division of Program Development and Management

Immediate Need for Personal Care/Consumer Directed Personal Assistance Services Informational Notice and Attestation Form

Attestation of Immediate Need for Personal Care Services/Consumer Directed Personal Assistance Services

I, ______________________________ (Name)

attest that I am in need of immediate Personal Care Services or Consumer Directed Personal Assistance Services.

I also attest that:

- No voluntary informal caregivers are available, able and willing to provide or continue to provide needed assistance to me;
- No home care services agency is providing needed assistance to me;
- Adaptive or specialized equipment or supplies including but not limited to bedside commodes, urinals, walkers or wheelchairs, are not in use to meet, or cannot meet, my need for assistance; and
- Third party insurance or Medicare benefits are not available to pay for needed assistance.

I certify that the information on this form is correct and complete to the best of my knowledge.

______________________________ ______________
SIGNATURE OF APPLICANT/ REPRESENTATIVE DATE SIGNED

Individuals Receiving Long Term Care Services in a Nursing Home or Hospital Setting

If you are receiving long term care services in a nursing home or a hospital setting and intend to return home, you may have your eligibility for Personal Care Services or Consumer Directed Personal Assistance Services processed more quickly. Follow the directions on the previous page and fill in the information requested below.

I am in a nursing home or a hospital setting and have a date set to return home on

____
DATE

Contact me or my legal representative by calling ______________________________.

DOH-5786 (11/22) Page 3 of 3

HIPAA – OCA – Official Form

OCA Official Form No.: 960

AUTHORIZATION FOR RELEASE OF HEALTH INFORMATION PURSUANT TO HIPAA

[This form has been approved by the New York State Department of Health]

Patient Name	Date of Birth	Social Security Number
Patient Address		

I, or my authorized representative, request that health information regarding my care and treatment be released as set forth on this form:

In accordance with New York State Law and the Privacy Rule of the Health Insurance Portability and Accountability Act of 1996 (HIPAA), I understand that:

1. This authorization may include disclosure of information relating to **ALCOHOL** and **DRUG ABUSE, MENTAL HEALTH TREATMENT**, except psychotherapy notes, and **CONFIDENTIAL HIV* RELATED INFORMATION** only if I place my initials on the appropriate line in Item 9(a). In the event the health information described below includes any of these types of information, and I initial the line on the box in Item 9(a), I specifically authorize release of such information to the person(s) indicated in Item 8.
2. If I am authorizing the release of HIV-related, alcohol or drug treatment, or mental health treatment information, the recipient is prohibited from redisclosing such information without my authorization unless permitted to do so under federal or state law. I understand that I have the right to request a list of people who may receive or use my HIV-related information without authorization. If I experience discrimination because of the release or disclosure of HIV-related information, I may contact the New York State Division of Human Rights at (212) 480-2493 or the New York City Commission of Human Rights at (212) 306-7450. These agencies are responsible for protecting my rights.
3. I have the right to revoke this authorization at any time by writing to the health care provider listed below. I understand that I may revoke this authorization except to the extent that action has already been taken based on this authorization.
4. I understand that signing this authorization is voluntary. My treatment, payment, enrollment in a health plan, or eligibility for benefits will not be conditioned upon my authorization of this disclosure.
5. Information disclosed under this authorization might be redisclosed by the recipient (except as noted above in Item 2), and this redisclosure may no longer be protected by federal or state law.
6. **THIS AUTHORIZATION DOES NOT AUTHORIZE YOU TO DISCUSS MY HEALTH INFORMATION OR MEDICAL CARE WITH ANYONE OTHER THAN THE ATTORNEY OR GOVERNMENTAL AGENCY SPECIFIED IN ITEM 9 (b).**

7. Name and address of health provider or entity to release this information:

8. Name and address of person(s) or category of person to whom this information will be sent:

9(a). Specific information to be released:

☐ Medical Record from (insert date) ________________ to (insert date) ________________

☐ Entire Medical Record, including patient histories, office notes (except psychotherapy notes), test results, radiology studies, films, referrals, consults, billing records, insurance records, and records sent to you by other health care providers.

☐ Other: ______________________________

____

Include: (*Indicate by Initialing*)

_______ **Alcohol/Drug Treatment**

_______ **Mental Health Information**

_______ **HIV-Related Information**

Authorization to Discuss Health Information

(b) ☐ By initialing here __________ I authorize ______________________________

Initials — Name of individual health care provider

to discuss my health information with my attorney, or a governmental agency, listed here:

____

(Attorney/Firm Name or Governmental Agency Name)

10. Reason for release of information: ☐ At request of individual ☐ Other:	11. Date or event on which this authorization will expire:
12. If not the patient, name of person signing form:	13. Authority to sign on behalf of patient:

All items on this form have been completed and my questions about this form have been answered. In addition, I have been provided a copy of the form.

______________________________ Date: ______________________________

Signature of patient or representative authorized by law.

* **Human Immunodeficiency Virus that causes AIDS. The New York State Public Health Law protects information which reasonably could identify someone as having HIV symptoms or infection and information regarding a person's contacts.**

Instructions for the Use
of the HIPAA-compliant Authorization Form to
Release Health Information Needed for Litigation

This form is the product of a collaborative process between the New York State Office of Court Administration, representatives of the medical provider community in New York, and the bench and bar, designed to produce a standard official form that complies with the privacy requirements of the federal Health Insurance Portability and Accountability Act ("HIPAA") and its implementing regulations, to be used to authorize the release of health information needed for litigation in New York State courts. It can, however, be used more broadly than this and be used before litigation has been commenced, or whenever counsel would find it useful.

The goal was to produce a standard HIPAA-compliant official form to obviate the current disputes which often take place as to whether health information requests made in the course of litigation meet the requirements of the HIPAA Privacy Rule. It should be noted, though, that the form is optional. This form may be filled out on line and downloaded to be signed by hand, or downloaded and filled out entirely on paper.

When filing out Item 11, which requests the date or event when the authorization will expire, the person filling out the form may designate an event such as "at the conclusion of my court case" or provide a specific date amount of time, such as "3 years from this date".

If a patient seeks to authorize the release of his or her entire medical record, but only from a certain date, the first two boxes in section 9(a) should both be checked, and the relevant date inserted on the first line containing the first box.

Chapter 10 | Appeals

Medicaid appeals come in a few different forms. There are several events in the lifespan of a home care case that may occasion an appeal. This chapter will address the situations we see most commonly: Immediate Needs appeals, New York Independent Assessor ("NYIA") appeals and MLTC appeals. The primary focus, however, will be the MLTC appeals which are the most procedurally cumbersome, and in which we are seeing the biggest increase.

A. Immediate Needs: Under certain circumstances it may be necessary to do an appeal in the immediate needs phase of the case (meaning when an application has been made through the expedited Immediate Needs process). If the client disagrees with the initial award of hours, the remedy would be a Fair Hearing. However, on a case-by-case basis, if we disagree with the number of hours awarded by the Local Department of Social Services (LDSS), we are often able to submit a new M11q (medical form used in the boroughs) or a doctor's letter and get the hours increased through advocacy.

Recently, although traditionally not that common, we now see cases getting stuck in between being approved for home care and having the care actually be put in place. This happens regularly now in high needs cases because the Home Care unit cannot find an agency to staff the case. It may also happen if something falls through the cracks somewhere in the process and for some reason the case isn't moving. We have seen this lately in the boroughs with the Community Alternative Systems Agencies ("CASAs") (I refer to these as Medicaid field offices when speaking with clients). This is something that has not been so much of a problem for several years, but it has become more common in the last year or so since we have been experiencing an aide shortage and since some reorganization has occurred in some of the CASA offices.

In this situation, the client has not yet been enrolled in an MLTC Plan, so MLTC is not involved. There has also technically not been an unfavorable decision or a "denial" from Medicaid (to the contrary, we have an approval), and some practitioners are concerned that a Fair Hearing is not necessarily an available remedy. However, the relevant federal statute states that a "State Plan for medical assistance must … provide for granting an opportunity for a fair hearing before the State agency to any individual whose claim for medical assistance under the Plan is denied **or is not acted upon with reasonable promptness**" [emphasis added].[3] We have scheduled Fair Hearings for these delays and have prevailed. Often we get the case settled without going forward with a complete hearing. I would argue that the "immediate need" in an Immediate Needs case is the need for the care (which is the very reason this procedure exists) – not merely the need for Medicaid approval, and that when a case drags on for months without care being put in place, this constitutes "not being acted upon with reasonable promptness".

This is not the first step we usually take, however. Thus far, we only resort to a Fair Hearing early on like this if we have not had any luck resolving the issues with the supervisors at CASA and the Home Care Services Program (HCSP). If unable to resolve the situation, then we will request an expedited Fair Hearing based on violation of the Immediate Needs time parameters.

---

[3] 42 U.S.C. 1396a(a)(3).

B. NYIA Assessments in Immediate Needs Cases: New York now requires two independent assessments to be conducted at the beginning of the process to determine if an individual is eligible for Personal Care Services (PCS) or Consumer Directed Personal Assistance Program (CDPAP) in New York. Upon receipt of an immediate needs home care application, the LDSS contacts NYIA and schedules two assessments: (1) a Community Health Assessment (CHA) to be completed by a nurse and (2) a Clinical Appointment (CA) to be completed by a physician or nurse practitioner. If this practitioner determines the individual is self-directing (or has someone who can direct the care) and has a stable medical condition, they will complete a Practitioner's Order (PO) advising the individual is eligible for MLTC.[4]

If the individual requires more than 12 hours/day, however, the case must be referred to an Independent Review Panel (IRP) for a high needs review. This panel has 6 days to advise the LDSS if the plan of care will maintain the patient's health and safety at home. If the IRP's determination is that health and safety cannot be maintained at home, the implication is that the individual needs to be forced into a nursing home. This decision is appealable. This appeal would be in the form of an Expedited Fair Hearing. We seem to be getting good results on these appeals so far. Unfortunately, this is at the expense of our clients, in both paying legal fees and paying privately for care pending the outcome of the appeal – not to mention experiencing the distress of fearing that they or their loved one may be forced into a nursing home.

C. MLTC: Unlike in fee-for-service Medicaid (e.g. Immediate Needs through the LDSS),the initial award of hours by an MLTC is not appealable at this time.

---

[4] GIS 22 MA/09

At this time, there are two common occasions when MLTC appeals are typically necessary:

1) When the Plan cuts the existing hours (including when the Plan reduces hours after the transition period from Immediate Needs to MLTC). In these cases, the Plan must give ten (10) days' written notice that it is reducing hours. (The effective date of the reduction must be at least 10 days after the notice date.) It is very important that the client request the Plan Appeal before the effective date so the client can get Aid to Continue, which means the hours will remain the same pending the outcome of the appeal.[5]

2) When an individual requests an increase in hours and the Plan denies the request. If we have the opportunity to get the client at the very beginning of the process, we advise that all requests for additional hours should be made in writing to the Plan and the request should be specific about how many hours are being requested (e.g. if looking for 24 hours/day, must indicate whether looking for live-in or 24-hour split-shift continuous care). The Plan will then do a new assessment and provide notice in writing of its decision. This notice will be either an Approval Notice or an Initial Adverse Determination if the request is denied or even partially denied. If the request is denied, the client has a right to appeal.

1. Internal Appeal (Plan Appeal)

This is the point at which a Plan Appeal must be exhausted. What that means is the client must appeal directly to the MLTC to reconsider its denial before proceeding to the next level of appeal. As a practical matter, we often see the Plans take the appeal request over the phone

---

[5] Goldberg v. Kelly, 397 U.S. 254 (1970)(holding the Due Process Clause of the Fourteenth Amendment requires an evidentiary hearing before recipient of certain government welfare benefits can be deprived of such benefits.

at the time the recipient is told by the Plan's care manager that the request has been denied. There is a procedure in the Plan's notice (the Initial Adverse Determination) that affords the recipient an expedited 72-hour appeal with the Plan if a letter from the patient's physician is provided, stating the patient's health or safety is in jeopardy if the appeal is not decided on an expedited basis. Otherwise, the Plan has 30 days to make a decision.[6] If the Plan fails to adhere to the notice and timing requirements, the enrollee is deemed to have exhausted the Plan Appeal process (called "deemed exhaustion")[7] and the member may proceed to the next level of appeal.

However, again as a practical matter, this Plan Appeal is often requested and conducted before the recipient even gets the Initial Adverse Determination. In many cases, it is decided in one day. The Plan will then call the recipient and advise that the appeal was denied - or that the Plan reconsidered and is approving the request. Assuming it was denied, thereafter, the recipient will receive both the Initial Adverse Determination (IAD) (which informs the client of the denial of the request) and the Final Adverse Determination (FAD) (which informs them of the denial on the Plan Appeal). If the client gets this information via a telephone call, it is imperative that they request the IAD, FAD and Uniform Assessment System – New York (UAS) (the Plan's assessment tool) be sent – or emailed - to them immediately.

Very often, our first contact with the client is after their Plan Appeal has already been denied. This is not tragic, though, because the Plan appeals are quite often denied, and the client gets this out of the way and retains us to do the appeals that we have a much better likelihood of winning. In fact, we sometimes advise the client to do this futile

[6] 438.408(b)(2).
[7] 438.408(c)(3).

verbal Plan Appeal and reach out once they've received the Plan's decision.

Our approach to the process

We approach the appeal process strategically, with an eye toward conserving the client's resources, getting the quickest result possible and yet preserving the right to have a second "bite at the apple" if we do not prevail.

The following is an example of a typical case and our strategies:

The client's daughter calls and says she requested more hours for her mom and the Plan denied the request. Right away we would need to know several facts:

1. How many hours were requested? If 24, did they request live-in or split shifts or did they not specify? If they did not specify, the Plan will characterize the request as live-in when it issues the IAD, and we will not be able to get any more hours than what *the Plan says the client asked for.*
2. Was the request made in writing?
3. Did they receive a written decision (in the form of an IAD)?
4. If so, did they request a Plan appeal?
5. If so, was a Plan appeal done? (At this point I might tell the client to go ahead and do it verbally over the phone to get it over with and advise the Plan to send the FAD immediately. This can save the client money in legal fees.)

Sometimes the client hasn't even received a decision yet, but the nurse doing the assessment or the case manager tells them they aren't eligible for the 24 hours. I've been shocked on a regular basis by some of the things the clients have been told. This is a really egregious practice by the Plans that we hear a lot.

Once we establish where the client is in the process, we ask for copies of the IAD, the FAD, the UAS (sometimes there are several) and all records the Plan has pertaining to the client (the Plan's Case File). In the meantime, we will plan our strategy. We have two options at this point: we can do an External Appeal or a Fair Hearing. All things being equal, I generally prefer to start with an External Appeal[8] (typically an expedited 72-hour appeal). The reason is that if we lose, we can go to a Fair Hearing[9] – whereas if we start out with a Fair Hearing and lose, we cannot then do an External Appeal.

Varshavsky Rights

If the request for increase was for 24-hour split shifts, the client may become a member of the class pursuant to the Varshavsky v. Perales[10] class action settlement. This entitles the client, upon proper documentation, to a homebound hearing. If a homebound hearing is not scheduled within 45 days, OTDA must direct that the increased care be put in place pending the outcome of the homebound hearing. So in addition to preparing an External Appeal, we will simultaneously request a homebound fair hearing, supported by a physician's letter stating the client cannot travel to a Fair Hearing without substantial hardship or medical detriment and, thus, requires a homebound hearing. We will also notify Varshavsky class counsel. This will get the clock ticking on the "Varshavsky relief". The state is permitted to hold a first hearing by phone. If the hearing is decided fully in the client's favor, there is no need for a home hearing. If a favorable decision is not issued within 45 days of the hearing request,

[8] 438.408 (f)(1)(ii).
[9] 438.408 (f)(2).
[10] 202 AD 2d 155 (1st Dept. 1994)

then the MLTC will be ordered to provide the increased hours pending the home hearing and subsequent decision.[11] It should be noted that the state's position at this time is that Varshavsky rights do not apply to Medicaid Advantage Plus Plans.

2. External Appeal

Once the Internal Appeal/Plan Appeal is exhausted, the client may file an External Appeal. An External Appeal is filed with the New York State Department of Financial Services (DFS) and must be referred to a reviewer that is independent of both the State and the Plan.[12]

Upon receipt of the proper documentation, the client is entitled to an expedited (72-hour) review. My experience has been that this time frame is strictly adhered to.

The following documentation should be submitted with the External Appeal:

- New York State External Appeal Application/Fast Track request form signed by doctor/provider (This form is available online and is also included in FAD letter)
- Letter from doctor advocating for the higher hours and stating that an expedited review is required so that the patient's health and safety will not be jeopardized
- Medical records from doctor (preferable but not required)
- The Plan's assessment or UAS
- Authorization Form
- Consent to Release of Records Form
- IAD
- FAD

---

[11] http://health.wnylc.com/health/afile/228/765/1/

[12] 438.408(c)(2).

- HIPAA Release
- Appeal Letter
- Any other information we have to support our client's request

Once we have all the above, we can draft a detailed appeal and submit the package.

You should get a fax from DFS on the same day acknowledging receipt and asking for any additional information or corrections. If the application is complete, DFS will send a fax advising which independent reviewer the case was sent to and giving the reviewer's contact information. The reviewer almost immediately faxes over a letter with a document request. We then immediately forward the entire package to the reviewer and follow up to confirm receipt.

The reviewer issues a decision within the 72 hours and we receive a copy of it from DFS. DFS simultaneously provides a copy of the decision to the Plan and, assuming we won, the Plan must provide the additional care immediately.

3. Fair Hearing

Some practitioners may prefer to go straight to a Fair Hearing after exhausting the Plan Appeal. Each case has its own factual and legal issues to analyze, and different practitioners have different strategies. The above represents how we typically approach a case in my office. Since COVID, the Office of Administrative Hearings (OAH) began conducting them telephonically. OAH calls a day before the scheduled hearing to confirm, and the Administrative Law Judge calls all parties at the time of the hearing. Evidence is to be submitted through OAH's new portal and served on the Office of Legal Affairs prior to the hearing.[13]

The Administrative Law Judge is required to render a written decision within 45 days.

Although not exhaustive, the aforementioned situations are what we've been seeing lately in my office. The number of appeals has increased dramatically. We are concerned daily about the safety and well-being of our home care clients in light of the cavalier way the Plans are treating their requests for care. In all our appeal cases thus far, the Plans' decisions have been in direct contradiction to much of the information contained in their own assessments – hence, the appeals are winnable. This suggests to me that the Plans have become ever more emboldened to put their bottom lines ahead of the population they serve without fear of reprisal. There are no financial penalties or sanctions. The only consequence to them is probably that the small percentage of people whose families can afford to fight them will win, but they get away with it with the vast majority of people who either do not know their rights or cannot afford lawyers. Although some of the home care clients have done prior transfers of assets or have families who can assist them financially, many, many people receiving home care through Medicaid are living at the poverty level and do not have family with resources. These people likely cannot afford to exercise their right to appeal. If the Plans continue to disregard the needs of these vulnerable elderly people and New York continues to allow it, the consequences to our seniors may be devastating. More scrutiny and oversight of the Plans is needed, and there should be a mechanism for sanctioning reckless determinations.

---

[13] https://upload.ny.gov/en-US/; *see* Office of Administrative Hearings (OAH) Transmittal 22-02, dated 9/1/22.

Sample External Appeal Checklist

STEPS/CHECKLIST

____ Get HIPAA, authorizing doctor/provider to disclose information to us (we may have in file if we did the application)

____ Get New York State External Appeal Application from materials received from Plan or online

____ Pull and complete all forms that require client's signature

- Consent to the Release of Records for New York State External Appeal,
- Appointment of Representative
- Authorization – Medicaid Managed Care
- HIPAA Release (for provider and DFS/Plan)

____ Email all forms together to client or POA for signature

____ Draft proposed letter for doctor based on medical information we have, advocating for the care and making required showing for expedited appeal and Varshavsky homebound hearing.

____ Email doctor proposed letter, request medical records with HIPAA Release; New York State External Appeal Application, which includes Physician's Attestation. Must follow up with doctor's office.

____ When have all the above documents, prepare the appeal. Go through each category in the IAD, FAD, all UASs and Plan's file and pull the information from the various documents. You will find information in the Plan's documents that supports our case. Always point out what our client's doctor stated in the doctor's letter.

____ Annex as exhibits all documents referred to in the appeal letter.

____ Fax over to DFS at 800-332-2729 the Appeal Letter, the External Appeal Request Form with the FAD and the forms signed by the client.

____ Call DFS at 888-990-3991 and inform them the appeal was just emailed over. They will check to make sure they have it and usually call us back. If they do not call to confirm, call them back.

____ Keep an eye out for fax from DFS asking any questions. When they consider the submission complete, they will send to reviewer for expedited review and email or fax us a letter with the reviewer's information.

____ Once DFS assigns case to a reviewer, email appeal with all exhibits (usually in 2 to 4 separate emails, titled "Email 1 of 4", etc.) to <u>the email address the Reviewer directs that it be sent to in the letter.</u>

I recently received a call from an existing client who filed an Immediate Needs application for his mother back in October, 2022, prior to the effective date of the requirement for the NYIA assessments. He then waited to hear from Medicaid and didn't hear anything. He researched online and determined that he should contact NYIA and schedule the two independent assessments. He did so and NYIA determined his mother was not eligible for care. When I asked why he scheduled NYIA assessments, he showed me something he had found on the internet, describing the process, and to a lay person, it made perfect sense. He did not really have any reason to know that this requirement was not in effect at the time he filed the application for his mother. He also did not, and would not, know that the LDSS arranges these assessments rather than the applicant. Now this client is stuck doing an appeal, which would have been completely unnecessary. Here is an example of a perfectly intelligent, capable family attempting to get care in place and unable to do so because of all the nuances and complexities of a very bureaucratic process.

-Lori Somekh

Chapter 11 | Waivered Programs

Nursing Home Transition and Diversion (NHTD)

Olmstead Plan: In its 1999 Olmstead v. L.C.[1] decision, the U.S. Supreme Court ruled that states, in accordance with the Americans With Disabilities Act ("ADA")[1], have an obligation to provide services to individuals with disabilities in the most integrated setting appropriate to their needs. The implementing regulations of the ADA define an integrated setting as one that "enables individuals with disabilities to interact with non-disabled persons to the fullest extent possible."

Accordingly, New York State developed a comprehensive Olmstead Implementation Plan to address integrated housing, employment, transportation, community services and other important issues.

In 2014, New York Association on Independent Living ("NYAIL") was selected by the Department of Health to coordinate the Open Doors Transition Center Project and Peer Outreach and Referral Program as part of State's Money Follows the Person ("MFP") program. The programs are funded through the MFP Federal Rebalancing Demonstration Grant.[1]

Open Doors

This program is sponsored by the Centers for Medicare and Medicaid Services ("CMS") and the New York State Department of Health. Rather than providing money directly to individuals, the MFP program funds the Open Doors program, which assists people living in nursing homes and other care facilities explore options for receiving services in the community.

"The Open Doors Rebalancing Demonstration Grant is a federal program created as part of the Deficit Reduction Act of 2006, and further extended as part of the Affordable Care Act, to assist states in shifting their Medicaid long-term care service and support system to support people with disabilities living in the community. The program seeks to promote rebalancing efforts toward which states increase the use of home and community-based services (HCBS) and reduce the use of institutionally based services."[14]

The Olmstead case and the resulting federal and state structures that were set up in compliance with this seminal case make it abundantly clear that the states are required to provide care in the community to the fullest extent possible. In my experience, the NHTD program is generally pretty good at doing that.

With the waivered programs, we have Regional Resource Development Centers ("RRDC"), located within Independent Living Centers throughout New York State. They work with nursing homes, managed care plans and Home and Community-Based Services to assist clients to identify and access needed supports, benefits, and services in the community. Open Doors serves as a bridge between

[14] Id.

pre-discharge planning and coordination in the facility and the delivery of medical and supportive services in the community.[15]

Since the NHTD clients must require a nursing home level of care, this program is typically utilized for high needs clients.

NHTD generally does not provide live-in care. If a client is transitioning from Immediate Needs or MLTC and already has been awarded live-in care, the NHTD program may permit that care to continue but they are more likely to authorize 24-hour split shift care.

Unlike traditional Medicaid home care, the NHTD program **does** permit oversight and supervision as stand-alone functions, without it being tied to a specific ADL. For example, a person with Alzheimer's or dementia can qualify even without the need for any physical disabilities if the person would be at risk if left alone.

The CDPAP program works a little differently with NHTD. The oversight and supervision stand-alone function cannot be performed by the CDPAP aide because that is not permitted in the CDPAP paradigm. Also, the aide cannot be an immediate family member – such as a parent, sibling or child. However, NHTD might offer to put the otherwise CDPAP aide through a training program to get PCA certified or Home and Community Supervisory Services (HCSS) certified so that aide can come under NHTD's criteria.

We have been utilizing this program more recently, in light of increasing problems in the MLTC world.

Service Coordination is required for all clients of the NHTD program. NHTD is authorized to provide all the services that traditional

---

[15]Id.

Medicaid home care can provide, plus 18 additional services. Those services are:

1. Home and Community Support Services (oversight and supervision)
2. Respite Services for 24 consecutive hours
3. Independent Living Skills Training and Development Services
4. Structured Day Program Services
5. Positive Behavioral Interventions and Support Services
6. Community Integration Counseling Service
7. Environmental Modifications Service
8. Environmental Modifications for Vehicles
9. Assistive Technology
10. Community Transitional Services
11. Moving Assistance
12. Congregate and Home Delivered Meals
13. Home Visits by Medical Personnel
14. Nutritional Counseling/Educational Services
15. Peer Mentoring
16. Respiratory Therapy
17. Wellness Counseling Service
18. Waiver Transportation

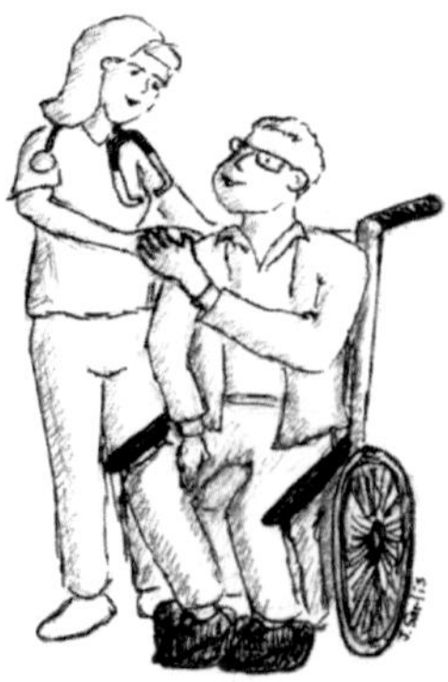

Chapter 12 | What if my loved one needs a nursing home after getting home care?

Because of the nature of this type of planning, where someone is already frail and in need of care, we often are not able to predict what the future brings in terms of the person's ongoing needs. We make the best decision we can with the information we have at the time, but in some situations, a person's condition deteriorates to the point where nursing home care becomes necessary. Without question, having proper care in the home can delay the need for nursing home. The question is: If we've gotten the person eligible for home care by doing transfers of assets (because there is no lookback period for home care at this time), and the person deteriorates and needs nursing home care within the 5-year lookback period for nursing home Medicaid, what do we do?

In this scenario, in order for the transfers to not be penalized, the transferred assets must be returned in their entirety. If a person returns any gifts made in the five (5) years before applying for nursing home Medicaid benefits, they will avoid being penalized for the full amount of the transfers. However, this puts them back in the position of being over-resourced (having too much money). There are then other planning techniques we can use, whereby we can still protect a portion of the assets. I like to call this "Plan B".

When this happens, we might use a Gift/Note Plan that allows us to preserve some of their assets in order to qualify for nursing home Medicaid. What we would do is give all the money back to mom or dad. Then we see what kind of expenses can be paid from her account off the top, such as pre-paid funerals, legal fees, outstanding bills, etc. Once we've spent as much of the money as possible on bills or exempt expenditures, we would then make a "gift" of roughly half of the remaining money. This gift would create a penalty period. During that penalty period, the nursing home must be privately paid. But before we get to that, we have to get the rest of the money out of the parent's name. In order to do that in a way that will not create a penalty period, we do a loan (let's say to the daughter) of the other half of the money. This way the parent is once again under the asset threshold. The daughter would then use that money to privately pay the nursing home for the duration of the penalty period. Technically, she would repay the parent each month and then write a check from the parent's account to the nursing home.

This was a gross over-simplification. There is a whole bunch of math and technical considerations that go into determining how much the gift and loan amounts will be. The actual calculations are beyond the scope of this book.

Chapter 13 | Medicaid Planning Techniques

Medicaid planning is an important part of ensuring that individuals receive the care and services they need without depleting their life's savings. There are several different ways to plan for Medicaid, depending on how far in advance you would like to begin your planning. Again, most people don't really think in terms of "planning for Medicaid." In fact, many people I speak to are confused by the concept. It might be helpful to think in terms of estate planning, and in the estate planning context, we're preparing for many of the possibilities that may lie ahead, such as: avoiding probate, possibly avoiding estate taxes (the things people usually do think of) and last but not least, avoiding losing your life's savings to long-term care. That is the Medicaid planning part.

The Administration on Aging estimates that at least 70% of people who are 65 years old today will require some form of long-term care in their lifetimes. (How sobering is that?) So, if you're not "broke" enough to qualify for Medicaid and not wealthy enough to pay for round-the-clock home health aides or a nursing home for an extended period of time, you will want to engage in Medicaid planning as a part of your estate planning.

When doing Medicaid planning, we first look at the possibility of exempt transfers. These are transfers of assets that, under certain circumstances, will not be penalized when determining an individual's eligibility for Medicaid benefits. Exempt transfers may include gifts to certain categories of family members or trusts set up for the benefit of a disabled person under 65 years old, for example.

The other category of transfers is non-exempt transfers. These are transfers of assets that are not considered exempt and will be taken into account when determining an individual's eligibility for nursing home Medicaid benefits. This is the category of transfers that will be penalized if done within five (5) years of entering a nursing home and applying for Medicaid. A penalty period is a period of time during which the applicant cannot receive Medicaid benefits even if they meet all other eligibility requirements. Non-exempt transfers may include outright transfers of assets to one or more of your children or transfers to certain types of trusts. It is essential to consider all potential outcomes before executing an any type of transfer. Seriously, not all transfers can be undone if you discover they weren't a good idea.

When planning for Medicaid, it may be beneficial to consider transferring assets to a Medicaid Asset Protection Trust ("MAPT"). This type of trust enables someone to transfer money or assets into an irrevocable trust that will not be counted as part of the applicant's estate when calculating Medicaid eligibility. You want to do this early, because there is the five (5) year look back period for nursing home Medicaid. Ideally, you want to be doing this well before the need for nursing home is imminent. This type of trust is also designed to avoid Medicaid estate recovery claims. There are certain formalities that must be adhered to when using the MAPT. The technical requirements of this type of trust is beyond the scope of this book, but you definitely want to have a conversation with your attorney about the feasibility of using this type of trust.

Personal services contracts ("PSC") are another form of Medicaid planning. Through a PSC, an individual can pay someone else to provide personal care services. This type of contract allows the recipient to maintain independence while still receiving certain types of services they need.

A PSC must meet certain criteria in order for it to be considered valid. This is essentially the senior compensating another person to perform certain specific services for them; for example, bookkeeping or bill paying, personal care, housekeeping or geriatric care management services. The compensation can be paid in advance in a lump sum, which enables the senior to get money transferred out of their name. However, the services must be itemized and calculated to use up the entire sum during the senior's life expectancy. Any amount not used must be paid back to the senior's estate upon the senior's death. We always advise clients to keep an ongoing log of the services provided. If the senior needs nursing home within 5 years of the transfer, Medicaid will scrutinize the log. Also, in that case, any unused portion must be paid back to the senior. It is important for the person being paid to perform the services to advise their accountant, because this is considered compensation and is ordinary taxable income. This is another planning technique you do not want to enter into without sound advice.

Yet another Medicaid planning vehicle is the Single Premium Immediate Annuity ("SPIA"). This product provides a way of converting a lump sum of money to an income stream, rendering the principle uncountable. This type of annuity must be irrevocable, non-assignable, actuarially sound and provide for equal monthly payments, with no deferrals or balloon payments. It must also name the State of New York as the primary beneficiary. This planning technique may be good for someone who does not have anyone they want to transfer assets to but needs to get the assets out of their name in order to qualify for Medicaid.

With the right planning, Medicaid can provide much-needed financial assistance for those in need of long-term care. From creating trusts and gifting assets, to using PSCs and SPIAs as strategies for protecting assets, there are a variety of options available when it comes to

Medicaid planning. By taking the time to understand these options and plan ahead, you can protect your hard-earned assets while ensuring that you receive the benefits you deserve.

Epilogue

It is our sincere hope that this information will provide some measure of guidance and comfort in your time of need. And always remember – we are here to assist if you need help.

Made in the USA
Las Vegas, NV
15 September 2026

22ee7069-2008-4a15-a5c5-57df5884a175R01